hotels • resorts • restaurants • vineyards • galleries

greecechic

text joe yogerst

thechiccollection

managing editor
francis dorai

executive editor
melisa teo

editor
li yuemin

assistant editor
meia ho

designers
nelani jinadasa • joanna poh

production manager
sin kam cheong

sales and marketing manager
antoine monod

first published in 2009 by
editions didier millet pte ltd
121 telok ayer street, #03-01
singapore 068590
telephone : +65.6324 9260
facsimile : +65.6324 9261
enquiries : edm@edmbooks.com.sg
website   : www.edmbooks.com
          www.thechiccollection.com

publishing partner
iforce communications s.a.
website: www.iforce.gr

©2009 editions didier millet pte ltd

Printed in Singapore.

isbn: 978-981-4217-96-5

Acknowledgements

We would like to acknowledge all those who have
made Greece Chic possible. Special thanks to
architects, Sophia Paraskevopoulou and George
Fatseas; Anna Mandonanakis of Helios Hotels; Gina
Mamidakis of BLUEGR; the Daskalantonakis family of
Classical and Grecotel; Costis Psychas of Perivolas;
Evangelos Gerovassiliou of Domaine Gerovassiliou;
Vassilis Tsarktsalis and Annegret Stamou of Ktima
Biblia Chora; Daphne Zoumboulakis of Zoumboulakis
Galleries, and to all who have lent their invaluable
knowledge and perspective to this publication.

1		5	6			11	13		14		19
	2	4		7			12			20	
			8	9	10	15	16	17	18	21	

COVER CAPTIONS:

1: *The hip Moet & Chandon Bar.*

2: *Athens is home to both old traditions
and cutting-edge trends.*

3: *The narrow Corinth Canal is one of
Greece's engineering marvels.*

4: *Years after the Athens Olympics, Greece's
tourist appeal still remains strong.*

5: *A statue of Alexander the Great looks over
the modern metropolis of Thessaloniki.*

6: *A statue of Pythagoras on Samos Island*

7: *Evzoni guards march to Syntagma Square
for the Changing of the Guard ceremony.*

8: *The lush vineyards of Kir-Yianni.*

9 AND 10: *From the streets of Athens to the
posh rooms of the Classical BabyGrand
Hotel, graffiti has become a way for
Greeks to express their creativity.*

11: *Greece is known for its sublime beaches.*

12: *Mykonos Blu reveals its playful side
through funky pop-art sculptures.*

13: *The iconic Erechtheion on the Acropolis.*

14: *Whitewashed churches are a distinctive
feature on Santorini.*

15: *Elounda Beach Palace is the epitome
of Mediterranean luxury.*

16: *Classical 2, Fashion House Hotel ensures
that its guests always live in style.*

17: *Scrumptious flavours abound at Hotel
Belvedere's Matsuhisa Mykonos.*

18: *The classic interior of Mykonos Blu.*

19: *The Temple of Poseidon at Cape Sounion.*

20: *At Classical King George Palace, ancient
art is given a contemporary twist.*

21: *Hundreds throng the grounds of Spiros
Louis, the Olympic Athletic Centre of Athens.*

THIS PAGE: *High fashion parades down the
catwalk during Athens Fashion Week.*

OPPOSITE: *The sun-bleached churches on Mykonos
morph into a surreal landscape in the evening.*

PAGE 2: *detail of a windmill at sunset*

PAGE 6: *At Perivolas, look out to gorgeous vistas
from the shaded comfort of one's pool.*

PAGE 8 AND 9: *The dramatic coastline of
Santorini at dusk.*

PAGE 150 AND 151: *At Amirandes, dining by the sea
is a truly magical affair.*

contents

introduction

The Acropolis bathed in the golden glow of sunset, the whitewashed windmills of Mykonos set against a sapphire sky, Zorba dancing the *syrtaki* on a rocky shore. With such images—both ancient and modern—dwelling in our collective consciousness, Greece has become one of those iconic places that many people have been to unconsciously even without ever physically setting foot on the land. Like an archaeological dig with many different layers, our knowledge of Greece accumulates over the years thanks to countless books, films, songs and history classes. And in this way, Alexander the Great and Aristotle Onassis, the Parthenon and *feta* cheese have become not only a part of everyone, but also timeless symbols of Greece.

Living up to the billing of 'great civilisation' has never been an easy task. In this respect, Greece has performed exceptionally throughout the ages, inspiring one society after another to follow in its cultural footsteps. What makes the country's formidable overseas image even more remarkable is the fact that even in European terms it's a relatively small nation—11 million people have been squeezed into an area barely larger than most American states.

Greece also stands out geographically, a constant contrast between land and water, hundreds of islands and a deeply indented mainland surrounded by celebrated bodies of water from the Aegean Sea to the Gulf of Corinth and the Strait of Salamis. Despite the waves of immigration from the Balkans in recent years and an increasing number of retirees from northern climes, Greece remains one of Europe's most homogeneous nations. More than 95 percent of the population is native Greek. And in that same vein, more than 95 percent would consider themselves Greek Orthodox even if they don't attend church on a regular basis.

a grecian holiday

Greece has attracted scores of travellers since the early 19th century, when Hellenism reached its peak and Athens became a regular stop on any grand tour of the eastern Mediterranean. It also became a popular retreat for European royals, with Queen Victoria, German Kaiser Wilhelm II and Empress Elisabeth of Austria becoming regular visitors to Corfu. In spite of its romantic image, Greek tourism only truly took off in the 1960s when two very different sets of tourists began flocking to the Greek isles: the upscale jet-setting circle and bohemian hippie backpackers.

Almost overnight, Greece blossomed into a hip destination for two very different crowds. This momentum continued to build up during the 1970s, as increasing numbers of the global elite and adventurous youths whiled away their summers on islands such as Mykonos, Santorini and Rhodes. While sun, sea and sand were undoubtedly the main attraction, Greece also earned a reputation for superb cuisine, wild nightlife and exquisite shopping. Cruise ships as well as posh private yachts arrived in no small numbers. And while traditional

THIS PAGE: *Approximately 20 million visitors set foot on Greek soil every year.*
OPPOSITE: *The volcanic cliffs of Santorini as seen from Thirasia island, located right in the middle of the caldera.*

Greece's tourist appeal reached a high point...

waterfront tavernas endure, there is no shortage these days of chic restaurants and designer hotels. The resurgence of Greece's tourist appeal reached a high point when the 2004 Summer Olympics sparked off an extreme makeover throughout Athens, the capital city.

in the beginning

Although many might perceive Greece's Golden Age (500–300 BC) as an ancient period within the long course of history, there are in reality even earlier settlers who inhabited the region that would later become the Hellenic heartland. The first people arrived around 350,000 years ago in modern Greece, and by Neolithic times they had evolved into simple farmers and fishermen living in modest villages. But all of that was about to change: there was to be an explosion of human enterprise the likes of which Earth has rarely seen.

Around 3200 BC, Bronze Age societies sprouted on the Aegean islands, in particular Crete, where the Minoan civilisation flourished for more than a thousand years. Greek-speaking peoples eventually migrated from the Caucasus to the mainland, where the Mycenaean civilisation was founded around 1600 BC. It was the Mycenaeans who laid the foundation for Greek civilisation and heralded the coming of the Classical Age, especially with regard to religion and folklore. Many Greek gods were derivations of Mycenaean originals and most scholars would agree that the legendary Trojan Wars—and nearly everything else that appears in the *Iliad*—took place in Mycenaean times.

With the collapse of the Mycenaean civilisation at the end of 1200 BC, Greece entered a 400-year period commonly known as the Dark Ages during which culture eroded and any semblance of ruling system collapsed. No one has ever been able to determine precisely why the Mycenaeans faded away, but it was likely a combination of foreign invasion, domestic strife and possibly famine or natural disasters.

the golden age

Just as mysterious is the reason Greek civilisation made a dramatic and widespread comeback around 800 BC. This pivotal turn of events arose from the emergence of vibrant mainland city-states such as Athens, Sparta, Thebes and Corinth. Fuelled by potent armies and robust political leaders, and well-schooled in

THIS PAGE: *A replica of a 3,500-year-old Minoan ship in the harbour at Chania on the island of Crete.*

OPPOSITE: *Beach umbrellas melt into a colourful mosaic along the coast of Rhodes.*

the arts, architecture and economics, each city-state soon rose to prominence, with much mutual rivalry and competition ensuing in the process. These independent city-states established colonies in Italy, Africa and Asia Minor, spreading Hellenic culture throughout the eastern Mediterranean.

Between 750–700 BC, Homer composed the *Odyssey* and the *Iliad*. Modern scholars may argue over whether Homer was a single person or a diverse collection of poets, but there is no disagreement that the Greek arts began to flourish during this time, with an outpouring of talent in poetry, drama, sculpture, ceramics and architecture. The ancient Olympic Games was founded during this era as well. By the late 6th century BC, the Greeks found themselves butting heads with another rapidly expanding civilisation—the Persians—who had already conquered a large majority of Asia Minor and had begun to set their sights on the Greek mainland. Twice the Persians sent massive invasion forces into Greece, resulting in iconic battles such as that of Marathon (490 BC), Thermopylae and Salamis (480 BC). Inspired by great military leaders such as Spartan king Leonidas (540–480 BC) and Athenian admiral Themistocles (524–459 BC), the Greeks eventually defeated the Persians and regained all of their land.

Victory in the Persian wars ushered in the Golden Age, a period of 150 years (480–330 BC) when ancient Greece reached its artistic, political, commercial and military peak. Despite constant rivalry between Sparta and Athens that frequently spilled over into warfare, the Greek city-states provided an incubator for many of the things we now think of as quintessentially Greek—drama, democracy, mathematics, philosophy as well as the great minds that fuelled this cultural explosion. Socrates (469–399 BC) contributed significantly to the realm of philosophy, while Herodotus' (484–425 BC) extensive accounts of the ancient world made him the 'Father of [Western] History'. Playwright Sophocles' (496–406 BC) dramatic masterpieces greatly influenced the development of theatre, while Pythagoras' (580–490 BC) geometric theorem is still considered a fundamental principle in the mathematics world today. Pericles (495–429 BC) consolidated Athenian democracy, while one of the largest ancient empires was created under the banner of young Alexander the Great (356–323 BC).

The Hellenistic empire under Alexander outlasted his untimely death by several centuries; it was a time when Greek language, culture, religion and architecture reached shores far beyond the eastern Mediterranean, and all the way to Afghanistan.

conquest and independence

The Roman victory over the Macedonians at Pydna in 168 BC and the sacking of Corinth in 146 BC marked the final downfall of ancient Greece and the end of Greek sovereignty for nearly two millennia. Greece would become a Roman province, nothing more than one of the many laurels the greater empire amassed. And while cities such as Athens and Corinth continued to thrive, they did so only under the unrelenting thumb of Rome. In addition to serving as the cultural inspiration for the upstart Romans, Greece also became a cradle of early Christianity.

By the 4th century AD, with the transfer of power from Rome to Constantinople, the Roman empire had evolved into the Byzantine realm—the primary political and cultural force in the eastern Mediterranean that would last well over 1100 years, from 330 AD until 1453. Based in Constantinople (modern Istanbul), the Byzantines nurtured their own distinctive art forms, architecture and Orthodox Christian customs which soon eclipsed older Greek traditions. The end of the Byzantine Empire saw Greece becoming easy prey for other rising external powers such as the Frankish Crusaders, whose religious zeal was exceeded by their greed for riches. While the Crusaders managed to make their presence felt around the margins of Greece, the Venetians, in particular, left their mark on the islands by controlling all major Greek ports and becoming the Mediterranean's most influential trading force.

But it was the Ottoman capture of Constantinople in 1453 AD that really changed things. Within a decade, the Ottomans had overrun all of the southern Balkans. Cultural brilliance in Greece once again took a back seat to basic survival. The country finally declared independence in 1821, after a bloody struggle against the Ottoman rule.

THIS PAGE: Olive groves comprise one of the most iconic of all Greek landscapes.

OPPOSITE: An imposing statue of Pythagoras on Samos island, where the mathematician cum philosopher was born and raised in ancient times.

One of the major goals of post-independence Greece was regaining as much former territory as possible, a task that would take more than a century. Britain gave back the Ionian Islands in 1864 and Thessaly was taken back from the Ottomans in the 1880s. The 1913 Balkan War brought Macedonia, Crete, Epirus and various northern Aegean islands back into the Greek fold. For a brief time after WW I, Greece also controlled a large part of Asia Minor (around present-day Izmir) and much of Thrace—until Turkish revolutionary Kemal Ataturk overthrew the Ottoman sultan and invaded the Greek enclaves along the Turkish coast.

Ataturk not only regained the old Ottoman lands, he also expelled more than 1.5 million ethnic Greeks from Asia Minor. The majority fled across the Aegean to mainland Greece, where the refugees swelled the populations of large cities such as Athens and Thessaloniki. Despite the hardships of forced relocation, these refugees would eventually prove themselves a force to be reckoned with—a great source of commercial, artistic, athletic and political talent that helped shape Greece throughout the remainder of the century.

modern greece

The Greece we know today took shape only after the end of the Nazi occupation in 1945. The nation began to edge into the 20th century, making the gradual—and sometimes painful—transition from agrarian to industrial economy, from ancient traditions to more modern ways and means. Rural-to-urban migration accelerated alongside island-to-mainland migration and Athens grew from a sleepy provincial town into a bustling sophisticated capital.

Contemporary Greece is now a fully functioning member of the European Union and NATO (North Alliance Treaty Organisation). Two major movements continue to shape Greek politics: the nation's ongoing rivalry with Turkey and the enduring struggle between the right and left on the home front—a political roller-coaster that has raced through numerous coups, a long military junta, the abolition of the monarchy and decades of civil strife, including the recent urban riots of 2008.

Yet somehow Greece continues to thrive. After years of languishing, the country's post-WW II economy took off and is now one of the top 30 performers in the world in terms of gross domestic product. Maritime shipping, agriculture, high-tech electronics and service industries are all prospering, while Greece has quietly become the primary foreign investor in the greater Balkans. But tourism, of course, remains the primary economic engine. More than 19 million people visit Greece each year, making it one of the world's top ten destinations. With an increasing number of resorts, attractions and archaeological finds surfacing all the time, there is no end in sight. As old Zorba told his young English apprentice, 'I have so much to tell you.' Greece certainly does.

THIS PAGE (FROM TOP): The Parthenon floats above the Christmas lights of downtown Athens; players from the Piraeus-based Olympiacos basketball club parade onto the court at Peace & Friendship Stadium.

OPPOSITE: The 2004 Summer Games infused Greece with a new spirit and a treasure of modern architecture, such as the futuristic Olympic Stadium in suburban Athens.

...a great source of commercial, artistic, athletic and political talent...

a cultural legacy

Greek art's magnificent materials, skilful craftsmanship and perfect proportions have always made looking at it a pleasure in its own right. Moving beyond Grecian shores, influences of Hellenic art can also be spotted in the works of renowned artists such as Picasso, Moore, Brancusi and Giacometti. From Gustav Klimt's Byzantine-like mosaics to modern theatre's reliance on ancient Greek theatre forms—much of the Western art world is derived from Greek invention through the ages.

The Minoan civilisation (3000–1100 BC) is best known for its 'Cycladic' marble sculptures of human figures whose simplified style appears oddly modern. Migrants, probably hailing from the Caucasus, brought with them the Greek language, the Olympian gods and new styles of pottery made on a wheel in the Middle Bronze Age, circa 2000 BC.

The Late Bronze Age, approximately 1400–1150 BC, was a time of legendary leaders: Agamemnon, Nestor, Odysseus, Theseus. Many excavated palaces of this period reveal murals depicting richly-dressed ladies and scenes of acrobats—both men and women—leaping over bulls. Trade with the Near East and Africa brought exotic luxury goods, and also introduced graceful octopi and other marine motifs to Greek-made pottery.

With the advent of the Dark Age (1150–776 BC), literacy and the civilisation's achievements disappeared. Known also as the Iron Age, pottery of this period is famous for its linear patterns and stylised silhouetted figures.

A new renaissance began quite literally when the first Olympic Games were held in 776 BC at Olympia. Another aspect of Greek revival was the return of reading and writing: the composition of the Homeric epics, which describe earlier heroic events of the Bronze Age, also dates to this time.

The art of the Archaic period, 7th–6th centuries BC, features *kouroi* and *korai*, large marble statues of young men and women, whose formal poses take after Egyptian sculpture. Eastern motifs such as sphinxes and griffins were popular in Archaic art, while floral designs, animals and realistic human figures found their way onto pottery.

The devastation of the Persian wars on Greece during the 6th and early 5th centuries BC was followed by rebuilding on a grand scale, especially in Athens. Sculpture of this Classical period strived for perfect proportions and idealised appearance, while introducing naturalistic movement. Proportion was sought in architecture too, and optical tricks—such as curved lines that appear straight—were employed to achieve the semblance of perfection, most famously evident in the Parthenon. Theatrical performance flourished as an art form, with both grand tragedies and bawdy comedies.

The Greek cultural world vastly expanded in the Hellenistic period through the conquests of Alexander the Great into Asia Minor, the Levant, and as far as Afghanistan, where Gandharan sculpture reveals strong Hellenistic influences.

The destruction of Athens by Roman generals in the 1st century BC did not diminish the prestige of Greek arts and literature: as the poet Horace put it, 'Captive Greece captured her savage conqueror, and brought the arts to rustic Rome.' Greek poems, plays and philosophical works copied on papyrus were read across the vast Roman Empire, while Greek-style theatres were built in Roman cities as far away as Spain and France.

The transfer of government from Rome to Constantinople in 330 AD, the adoption of Christianity as the official state religion, and barbarian incursions in the west during the 4th and 5th centuries began the cultural and political transformation of the Roman Empire into what we call Byzantium.

In the Byzantine period, Greece as a province was ruled from Constantinople from 330 AD until the sack of Constantinople by the Fourth Crusade in 1204. After 1204, Greece was divided into principalities under Frankish domination, and subsequently Catalan and Venetian rule, though a few Byzantine princes held out in Epirus and Mistra.

Byzantine art saw both Christian and pagan subjects depicted in mosaic, ivory and book illustrations. Perhaps the best-known contribution of Byzantine art is the icon or religious portrait image. The term iconoclasm was invented to denote the bitter philosophical conflict— at a time of military losses to Muslim Arabs in the 8th and 9th centuries— over whether or not it was appropriate for Christians to create and worship pictorial depictions of Christ. Innumerable works of art were destroyed before the conflict was resolved, and icon-worship was

only restored in the 9th century, a period which coincided with military gains against the Arabs and Slavs, as well as a renewal of artistic and literary activity.

The capture of Constantinople in 1453 by the Ottomans restored a strong central government in that city, and in the Ottoman period Greece once again became part of a vast multi-ethnic empire. Ottoman buildings in Greece include baths derived from Romano-Byzantine models, and domed mosques which echo the architecture of St Sophia.

Under Ottoman rule, the country saw the erection of many mosques, while countless Christian churches were converted into Islamic places of worship.

Today, the diverse monuments of Greece now include pagan temples, Christian churches, Roman baths, Gothic castles, Turkish mosques and Jewish synagogues, and belong to a cultural continuum which extends far beyond the country's borders.

athens
the archaeological parks

At the heart of Athens, a zone of green parks and pedestrian streets encircles the Acropolis, linking it with the **Agora**, **Kerameikos** and **Temple of Olympian Zeus**. The **Acropolis**, a fortified citadel since the Bronze Age, was in antiquity the greatest sanctuary of Athena, goddess of wisdom, and encompassed several important structures.

The **Parthenon** was built under Pericles in the mid-5th century BC to replace a temple destroyed by the Persians. Converted to an Orthodox

THIS PAGE (FROM TOP): The monastery of the Virgin Hozoviotissa on Amorgos; a flute player and dancer cavort on a 6th-century BC drinking cup.

OPPOSITE: Recovered from a shipwreck at Cape Artemision, the 'Horse and Jockey of Artemision' (circa 140 BC) now resides at the National Archaeological Museum in Athens.

a cultural legacy

church in 5th century AD, to a Catholic church in the 13th century by the Crusaders, and to a mosque in the 15th century by the Ottomans, the marble building survived intact as a house of worship until 1687 when Venetian forces attacked with cannon fire, igniting gunpowder stored inside by the defending Ottomans.

The **Erechtheion** housed several cults, including commemoration of the contest between Athena and sea-god Poseidon for the city: her gift of an olive tree was considered more useful than his saltwater spring. The tiny **Temple of Nike** (Temple of Victory) honours Athena's role in war. Near the entrance to the Acropolis site is the stony outcrop of the

Areopagus, where St Paul is said to have preached to the Athenians. A narrow path passes sacred caves on the north slope of the Acropolis dedicated to Zeus, Aphrodite and Pan.

Just north of the Acropolis is the Agora (Adrianou Street), the central square, seat of government and marketplace of classical Athens. Democracy was first practised here from 508 BC, and tools of the first democracy—secret ballots and *ostraka* (votes anonymously written on broken pieces of pottery)—are on display in the Agora Museum. Philosophers, including Socrates, taught here, and splendid public buildings and works of art stood around the square.

Overlooking the Agora is the 5th-century BC **Temple of Hephaistos**, nearly intact since the middle ages when it was a church of St George. The **Agora Museum** (24 Adrianou Street) is situated in the Stoa of Attalos, built by King Attalos II of Pergamon in 159 BC and restored by the American School of Classical Studies. On the other side of the street, the Agora excavations continue during summer months.

Along Ermou Street is the **Kerameikos**, the burial ground of ancient Athens. Funerary sculpture and offerings are displayed in the **Kerameikos Museum** (148 Ermou Street). Nearby are the **Benaki Museum of Islamic Art** and the 11th-century Church of Asomatoi.

monastiraki and the central market

Monastiraki Square, which takes its name from the 15th-century Church of the Pantanassa, was, in Ottoman times, the bazaar of the city. Overlooking the square, the 18th-century **Tzisdarakis Mosque** is now a museum of traditional pottery. Next door is the monumental entrance of **Hadrian's Library**, built in the 2nd century AD when Athens was primarily a centre for education.

There are two lovely Byzantine churches nearby: 12th-century **Panagia Gorgoepikoos** in Mitropoleos Square, next to the Metropolitan Cathedral of Athens, and 11th-century **Kapnikarea** in the middle of Ermou Street. A few *souvlaki* (meat and vegetable skewers) restaurants, antique shops and sandal shops remain on Mitropoleos and Pandrossou streets; however, one is hard-pressed to find local or traditional goods. A more authentic Middle Eastern flavour may be found along Athinas Street, with shops selling spices, incense, olives and cheese in the neighbourhood of the central meat and fish markets.

the roman agora and plaka

East of the Agora, the **Gate of Athena Archegetis** leads to the **Roman Agora** (corner of Pelopida and Eolou streets), a great colonnaded square built under Julius Caesar and Augustus in the late 1st century BC. Here, the **Tower of the Winds**—which was copied all over Western Europe in the 19th century—was built as a water-clock for the Roman marketplace, and reused by the whirling dervishes in the Ottoman period.

The **Fethiye Mosque** (corner of Panos and Pelopida streets) was built by the Ottomans in 1456 over the foundations of a church. The **Bath House of the Winds** (8 Kyrristou Street) is now a museum devoted to the tradition of public baths which lasted from antiquity to Ottoman times. In summer, the **Museum of Greek Musical Instruments** (1–3 Diogenous Street) hosts concerts in a lovely courtyard.

The historic district of **Plaka** is closed to cars except for a one-way loop, from Lysikratous to Tripodon streets and out again on Navarchou Nikodemou Street. At the end of Lysikratous Street, the **choragic monument of Lysicrates** (circa 334 BC) was reused as the library of a Capuchin monastery and frequented by Lord Byron. On Kydathenaion Street is the **Museum of Greek Folk Art** (17 Kydathenaion Street), with embroideries, costumes, ceramics and woodwork. The nearby **Jewish Museum** (39 Nikis Street) tells the story of the city's Jewish community. The 11th-century **Sotira Lykodemou** church on Philhellenon Street is now the Russian church of Athens.

Climb up past Plaka to explore **Anaphiotika**, the labyrinthine whitewashed village suspended high above the modern urban sprawl. Or walk down Lysikratous Street past the 12th-century **Aghia Ekaterini** (church of St Catherine) to **Hadrian's Arch** and the **Temple of Olympian Zeus**, completed under Hadrian in the 2nd century AD. Beyond it is the **Panathenaic Stadium**, originally constructed in 330 BC and restored for the first modern Olympics in 1896.

THIS PAGE (FROM TOP): The National Museum of Archaeology continue to be a great draw for tourists; The Caryatid Porch of the Erechtheion on the Acropolis.

OPPOSITE (FROM TOP): Much of ancient Greek sculpture is characterised by fine details and life-like proportions; a Cycladic figure and vessels.

a cultural legacy

The pedestrian promenade below the south slope of the Acropolis (Dionysiou Areopagitou and Apostolou Pavlou streets) leads to the **New Acropolis Museum** (2–4 Makryianni Street), built to house sculptures from the surrounding temples; the **Theatre of Dionysus**, where works by Aeschylus, Sophocles and Euripides were first performed; and the Roman theatre, **Herodes Atticus Amphitheatre**, where performances are staged in summer. Creations in gold are on display at the **Ilias Lalaounis Jewellery Museum** (12 Kallisperi Street and Karyatidon Street).

downtown

Syntagma Square, dominated by Parliament, is the modern centre of Athens. From here, a stroll along Vasilissis Sophias Avenue takes one to many of the city's museums.

For an overview of 5,000 years of Greek art, including jewellery, costume and interiors, visit the **Benaki Museum** (1 Koumbari Street at Vasilissis Sophias Avenue). Starkly geometric marble figurines, 4,000 to 5,000 years old, are the stars of the **Museum of Cycladic Art—Nicholas P Goulandris Foundation** (4 Neophytou Douka Street). Icons, as well as carved marbles, jewels, textiles and mosaics are on display at the ultra-modern **Byzantine and Christian Museum** (22 Vasilissis Sophia Avenue).

Works by modern Greek artists are showcased at the **National Gallery** (1 Michalakopoulou Street and 50 Vasileos Konstantinou Street). Over the columns of the **Gennadius Library** (61 Souidias Street) are the words of the orator Isocrates: 'all who share in our culture may be called

Greeks.' The library's collection includes Byron memorabilia, early travel books and Ottoman documents.

between syntagma and the omonoia area

A short distance from Syntagma Square along Stadiou Street is the **Museum of the City of Athens** (5–7 Paparrigopoulou Street, Klafthmonos Square), housed in King Otto's first residence, with memorabilia of the last years of Ottoman rule and the birth of modern Greece. Don't miss early travellers' books and a 1674 painting depicting the Acropolis, complete with the Parthenon before it was destroyed by an explosion

In the same square is the Church of the two Saints Theodore, dated 1065. Greek coins of all periods are found in the collection of the **Numismatic Museum Athens** (12 Panepistimiou Street), located in the neoclassical home of pioneering archaeologist Heinrich Schliemann.

Ancient treasures from all over Greece are gathered at the **National Archaeological Museum** (44 Patission Street), a must-see for any visitor. Next door is the highly interesting **Epigraphical Museum** (1 Tositsa Street), where text and objects are combined in inscriptions carved on stone for public display, including laws, honorific decrees, historical accounts and gravestones.

the coast

In **Piraeus Archaeological Museum** (31 Charilaou Trikoupi Street) are extraordinary over-life-sized bronze statues with even the eyelashes preserved. In and around **Zea Harbour** are preserved remains of the ancient ship sheds of the Athenian navy. A great mound marks the graves of those who fell at **Marathon**; a small museum (114 Plataion Street) has finds from the battlefield. The **Temple of Poseidon** at Cape Sounion, still a beacon to travellers, is flooded with crowds at sunset.

central greece

Sacred to Apollo, god of arts and music, who frequented Mount Parnassus with his entourage of Muses, **Delphi** was considered the navel of the world. Pilgrims visited the mountainside sanctuary to consult the Delphic Oracle. A short drive from Delphi is the spectacular 10th–11th century Byzantine monastery of **Hosios Loukas**. **Thebes**, said to have been founded by a Phoenician, was home to Oedipus; its **Archaeological Museum** (1 Threpsiadou Street, Keramopoullou Square) has rich finds from the Bronze Age. Near Mount Pelion is the city of Volos, with an excellent **Archaeological Museum** (1 Athanasaki Street) housing finds from the Stone Age site of Sesklo.

the peloponnese

Corinth strategically guards the narrow isthmus which connects the Peloponnese with mainland Greece. Utterly destroyed in 146 AD by the Roman general Mummius, the city revived in Late Antiquity.

In contrast to rival Athens, **Sparta** was renowned more for discipline and self-sacrificing heroism than for its literature or monuments. Finds from the region are displayed at the **Sparta Archaeological Museum**.

Also worth a visit is the **Museum of the Olive and Greek Olive Oil** (129 Othonos-Amalias Street). Atop a conical hill nearby, the late Byzantine town of **Mistra**, has frescoed churches and a Crusader castle. The medieval offshore citadel of Monemvasia has churches of the 13th century.

Epidaurus hosts performances at its two ancient theatres during the summer festival. The hilltop **citadel of Mycenae**, 'rich in gold', was home of the Bronze Age King Agamemnon. Finds from the royal graves are kept in the National Archaeological Museum in Athens; there is also an on-site museum—the **Mycenae Archaeological Museum**. Nafplion is

a cultural legacy

a lovely seaside town dominated by the Venetian Palamedion fortress. The **Napflio Archaeological Museum** is on Syntagma Square; for artefacts of more recent date visit the **Peloponnesian Folklore Foundation** (1 Vas Alexandras Street).

Olympia's stadium, gymnasium and hippodrome were home to the original Olympic Games. Its temple of Zeus housed a gold-and-ivory statue, one of Seven Wonders of the ancient world. **Pylos** is the site of the Bronze Age palace of King Nestor, the sage elder statesman of the *Iliad*. The sheltered bay saw the famous naval battles of Sphakteria (425 BC) and Navarino (1827 AD). Both Olympia and Pylos boast museums that may be of interest to travellers.

The Lion of St Mark adorns the Venetian fortresses of **Koroni** and **Methoni**, strategic ports on the way to Crete, Cyprus and the Levant. Near Kalamata are the impressive remains of the ancient city of **Messine**.

The **Mani** peninsula, with its mountainous, savagely dramatic landscape, was famous in more recent times for feuds which fostered the distinctive tower architecture of Maniote villages.

northern greece

Thessaloniki, on the Egnatian Way which led from Rome to Constantinople, has well-preserved Late Roman monuments. Of note are the 5th-century **Church of St Demetrius**—patron of the city—and the **Rotonda**, built as a mausoleum, converted to the Church of St George and later a mosque. Visit the prize-winning new **Byzantine Museum** (2 Stratou Avenue) and the **Thessaloniki Archaeological Museum** (6 Manoli Andronikou Street). The **Jewish History Centre** (24 Tsimiski Street) preserves the memory of the city's Jewish community, which welcomed refugees from the Spanish Inquisition but was later decimated under German occupation.

At **Vergina** is the splendid tomb of King Philip II, father of Alexander the Great. **Pella**, birthplace of Alexander, was the capital of ancient Macedonia; finds at the **Pella Archaeological Museum** include mosaic floors. At the foot of Mount Olympus is the archaeological site of **Dion**, with its **shrine of Zeus**.

Not far from **Kavala**, with its monumental aqueduct built by Sultan Suleiman the Magnificent, is the site of **Philippi**, with ruined Late Antique churches.

The lakeside town of **Ioannina**, home of Ali Pasha, has a picturesque fortress whose mosque houses the **Municipal Museum**, with costumes of the Christian, Muslim and Jewish communities. There are 16th-century frescoed churches situated on the island in the lake. **Arta**, capital of the Despotate of the Epirus, has a haunted Ottoman bridge and beautiful 13th-century churches, including the **Paregoritissa**.

ionian islands

A strong Italian influence sets the Ionian islands apart from those east of the mainland. **Corfu Town** with its arcaded streets and cricket ground is home to the **Antivouniotissa Byzantine Museum** (Arseniou Street), the **Archaeological Museum**

(Dimokratias Street), and, in a neoclassical palace, the **Asian Art Museum** (Kapodistriou Street).

Verdant **Ithaca** was the home of Odysseus; the location of his palace has yet to be found. An earthquake in 1953 devastated Cephalonia island, but the town of **Fiskardo** with its crusader fortress escaped. Visit the **Archaeological Museum** in Argostoli (G Vergoti Street). **Zakynthos**, famous for its currants, has some of the most spectacular beaches in Greece with protected breeding-grounds for the Karetta karetta sea turtle.

aegean archipelago

Complement the hedonism of Mykonos with an excursion to pristine **Delos**, island birthplace of Apollo and his sister Artemis. In **Paros**, see sculptures in white island marble at the **Archaeological Museum** in Paroikia and, next door, the **6th-century Church of the Virgin Hekatontapyliani**.

Naxos was capital of the Venetian Duchy of the Archipelago. See marble Cycladic figurines in the **Archaeological Museum**, and the three giant Archaic marble *kouroi* in the countryside. The Venus de Milo is no longer in residence on the volcanic island of **Milos**, but there is a replica at the **Archaeological Museum** in Plaka—and many others for sale on the island.

Samos has monuments of the Archaic period: the **temple of Hera** and **aqueduct of Eupalinos** and impressive marble *kouroi* displayed in the **Archaeological Museum** in Vathy. Visitors to the holy island of **Patmos** must bear in mind that it is still a place of Christian pilgrimage and a centre of Orthodox monasticism,

with an 11th-century **Monastery of St John the Theologian** and other convents and hermitages.

Rhodes—famed in antiquity for the Colossus—was, in the Middle Ages, the seat of the Knights Hospitaller. Medieval buildings house the **Archaeological Museum** (Megalou Alexandrou Square) and the museum in the **Palace of the Grand Master** (Ippoton Street).

Crete, the birthplace of Zeus, was also the home of the Minotaur and its labyrinth—legends which arose around the Bronze Age **Palace of King Minos** at Knossos. Finds from the site are displayed at the **Herakleion Archaeological Museum** (Xanthoudidou and Chatzidaki streets). The picturesque port of **Hania** has Venetian and Ottoman monuments and fortifications.

THIS PAGE (FROM TOP): The Terrace of the Lions flanks the Sacred Way on Delos; Despite being a Christian stronghold, Rhodes also features stunning examples of Islamic architecture such as the Mosque of Suleiman; the main courtyard in the Palace of the Grand Master in Rhodes.

OPPOSITE (FROM TOP): Remains of an early 18th-century Venetian arsenal in the town of Gouvia on Corfu; an impressive ancient floor mosaic amid the ruins of Pella.

made in greece

As one of the great crossroads of the Mediterranean basin, Greece has been a trading centre for more than 7,000 years. Many of the items that the ancient Greeks manufactured and traded with the rest of the world—jewellery, ceramics and carpets, wine and olive oil, art and religious icons—remain the most sought-after products today.

Athens is without doubt the best place in Greece for a shopping spree, especially the posh **Kolonaki neighbourhood** with its fashion boutiques and art galleries. The upmarket holiday isles like **Mykonos**, **Santorini**, **Rhodes** and **Corfu** are also perfect for a splurge, with an eclectic array of shops that cater to jet-set visitors and well-heeled residents. But some of the best bargains, especially locally made items, are found off the tourist track, in bustling cities such as **Thessaloniki** and **Patras**, and smaller regional centres such as **Nafplion** in the Peloponnese and **Iraklion** on Crete, where price tags are aimed at modest local shoppers rather than wealthy cruise ship passengers.

greek haute couture

Athens may not have reached the same exalted heights as Paris and Milan, but it's not half bad when it comes to homegrown *haute couture*. **Nikos & Takis** have been designing one-off frocks and upscale *prêt a porter* since 1962, when they first collaborated. Among the famous femmes the duo has clad in the past are Sofia Loren, Elizabeth Taylor, Maria Callas and Jackie Onassis. Handwoven fabric and muslin were their original forte, but they have

since branched out. Their **flagship boutique** (26 Skoufa Street, Kolonaki) is in Athens but they also have branches in suburban Peristeri, Thessaloniki and Rhodes.

Sophia Kokosalaki has earned a well-deserved reputation far beyond Greece for her edgy black-and-white frocks, some of them modish in a 1960s way and others almost throwbacks to classical Grecian designs. She also designed the 2004 Olympics closing ceremony outfits for the Greek National Team. The **Bettina boutique** (40 Anagnostopoulou Street, Kolonaki) in Athens is the best place to pick up an original Kokosalaki frock.

Although he originally made his name on chic wedding dresses and party outfits, **Michalis Aslanis** has gone off on all sorts of different design tangents. This versatile Greek designer has applied his unique vision to items ranging from intricate bed linens, curtains, tablecloths and towels, to irreverent lighting and furniture pieces, an entire baby collection and even porcelain dinner sets. Although Aslanis' creations can be found in lifestyle boutiques throughout Greece, his flagship outlet is situated in the **Moschato area** of south Athens (Lefkados 2B and Artis streets).

jewellery + accessories

Greece has produced exquisite trinkets for thousands of years, but the modern jewellery industry traces its roots to the late 19th century, when Sotirios Voulgaris established a modest jewellery store in the village of Paramythia, in the Epirus region of northwestern Greece. Sotirios later moved on to Corfu and then Italy, where he changed his name to the Latinised 'Bulgari'. In doing so, he not only established one of the world's greatest luxury brands, but also laid the foundation for Greece's thriving modern jewellery scene. **Bulgari**'s flagship boutique is located in the heart of the fashionable Kolonaki district (8 Voukourestiou Street).

Another notable jeweller is **Kessaris** (7 Panapistimiou Street), whose elegant, finely crafted jewel pieces have been adorning dignitaries, socialites and celebrities since 1965.

Ilias Lalaounis is perhaps Greece's best known contemporary goldsmith. Born in 1920, Ilias designed more than 50 separate golden collections until the year 2000, when he finally retired. More than 4,000 of his pieces—many of them based on ancient Neolithic, Mycenaean and Byzantine designs—are on display in the **Ilias Lalaounis Jewellery Museum** (12 Kallisperi and Karyatidon streets, Acropolis).

The museum also houses a genuine workshop where visitors can watch raw gold being shaped into exquisite earrings, bracelets and necklaces. In addition, there's a Lalaounis boutique in Kolonaki (6 Panepistimiou Street) and another in Rhodes (Alexander Square, Old Town).

Another legendary name in Greek jewellery is **Zolotas**, founded in 1895 by Efthimios Zolotas, incidentally also the workshop where Lalaounis apprenticed before striking out on his own. Also known for its modern takes on ancient Hellenic jewellery, Zolotas has fashioned custom gold pieces for the likes of style icons such as Princess Grace of Monaco. Nowadays

Zolotas specialises in contemporary 18 and 22 carat gold pieces, many of them set with precious gemstones (10 Panepistimiou Street, Kolonaki).

The gold-and-semi-precious gemstone creations of **Elena Votsi** (7 Xanthou Street, Kolonaki) and **Katerina Psoma** (www.katerinapsoma.com) bring edgy sophistication to the Greek jewellery industry. Their irreverent and whimsical pieces are highly sought after by fashionistas world-wide.

The more cosmopolitan islands also offer a good selection of custom jewellers, such as the stylish **Kostas Antoniou** on Santorini (Ayiou Ioannou Street, Fira) which offer modern gold pieces based on ancient Minoan designs. On the island of Corfu, **Alexandra** (18 Sokratous Street, Corfu Town) makes gold, silver and platinum jewellery, frames and trays.

art + icons

It may no longer be possible to bargain for ancient masterpieces, but modern Greek painting, sculpture and photography are among the finest in Europe and highly prized by serious collectors both at home and abroad. Works by 20th-century masters such as avant-garde sculptor **Takis**, abstract expressionist **Theodoros Stamos**, mixed media maestro **Jannis Kounellis** and painter **Yiannis Moralis** now fetch a small fortune and are normally only available at auctions overseas. But like everywhere else, the work of rising artists tend to be more affordable and readily available at domestic galleries.

As with fashion and jewellery, the capital's modern art scene is heavily concentrated in the Kolonaki district, which boasts more than a

THIS PAGE (FROM TOP): Classical influence is clearly evident in this creation at a spring/summer fashion show at the Athens Technopolis; a common trend, modern Greek jewellery often incorporates antique motifs into its designs; startling local pop art is the forte of the cutting-edge Astrolavos galleries in Kolonaki district, Athens.

OPPOSITE: The annual Fashion Week in Athens brings out the best of contemporary Greek design.

dozen fine galleries. A mover and shaker in the Greek art world for nearly a century, **Zoumboulakis Galleries** flaunts a wide selection of original painting and sculpture, as well as silk screens, posters and signed numbered prints by many of Greece's greatest living artists. Zoumboulakis has several branches, including the main gallery at 20 Kolonaki Square. Other stalwarts of the Athens modern art scene include the abstract-heavy **Gallery Nees Morfes** (9 Valaoritou Street, Kolonaki) and funky, pop art-filled **Astrolavos Galleries** (branches at 11 Irodotou Street and 11 Xanthippou Street, Kolonaki).

Contemporary art is also available at galleries in Mykonos, Santorini, Rhodes and Corfu. Thessaloniki also has a rapidly growing arts scene and an ever-expanding menu of galleries. **Donopoulos International Fine Arts** (56 Andreou Georgiou Street) stocks a large selection of contemporary artworks, sculpture and photography by up and-coming young Greek artists.

Given the fact that it's illegal to export artwork older than a century without a licence, ancient artefacts and icons are not allowed to be sold in Greece. However, there is a thriving trade in antique furniture, books and coins, which are more easily exported.

The capital's antique shops cluster around **Syntagma Square** and the **Monastiraki neighbourhood**. **Antiqua** (2 Amalias Avenue, Syntagma) is one of the more reputable dealers, and also one of the more diverse. Offering a vast selection of old furniture and carpets, stamps and coins, books and prints, and much more, this antiques paradise is a wonderful place to browse, even if one doesn't buy.

spirits + edible delights

From exclusive wineries to waterfront tavernas, there is certainly no shortage of opportunity to buy fine wines and spirits in Greece. The three celebrated Greek spirits—*ouzo*, *metaxa* and *tsipouro*—are all grape-based. The trick is finding a place with a broad selection of premium brands and someone who can explain the subtle differences. **Angelo**, the *ouzo* shop (120 Adrianou Street, Plaka) and the wonderfully decadent **Oino-Pnévmata** (9A Irakleitou Street, Kolonaki) are two such places, stocking many of the latest, popular Greek vintages.

Given their long history of being shipped all across the Mediterranean, many Greek food products also travel well. The most atmospheric place to shop for cheese, olives and olive oil, pistachios, honey, *halva* candy and other farm products is the central market in any Greek city or town.

Another good source is **Green Farm**, an organic supermarket chain with outlets in Athens (13 Dimokritou Street, Kolonaki), Piraeus, Pátra, Ioánnina and elsewhere. Among the many delights at Green Farm are *feta* and *myzithra* cheese, olive paté and olive paste, honey-sesame bars, sun-dried tomatoes, jams and marmalades, and *kritharaki* pasta.

Another great culinary memento is **Loumidis Papagalos coffee**, similar to traditional Turkish coffee, brewed in a small brass pot and served in tiny cups with what seems to be an inch of sugar and sediment at the bottom. There's a **Loumidis Papagalos** boutique near Omonia Square in Athens (106 Aiolou Street).

Aristokratikón in Athens (9 Karagiórgi Servías, Syntagma) makes a wide range of gourmet Greek sweets such as handcrafted chocolates, marzipan delights and caramel pistachios. There are also branches in suburban Kifissia and Glyfada.

odds + ends

Museum shops are generally the best places to find reproduction amphorae, icons, busts and decorative plates. These souvenirs are easily found all over Greece, but good replicas can be found in museum shops in downtown Nafplion such as the **Komboloi Museum shop** (25 Staikopoulou Street), which sells reproduction amulets and worry beads (*kombolói*). On the island of Rhodes, try the **Ministry of Culture Museum Reproduction Shop** (Ipitou Street) for reproduction sculptures, vases, tiles and friezes.

A wide range of handicrafts are also available in Thessaloniki. The **old Turkish bazaar** shelters shops selling carpets, copperware and other collectables. The 15th-century **Bezesteni** (Venizelou and Solomou streets) is also worth visiting, with its warren of lanes beneath six old Turkish domes.

Royal Oriental Carpets (33 Apellou Street) in Rhodes offers an impressive array of rugs, vases and decorative trinkets. They also have a shop in Athens (33 N. Nikodemou Street, Plaka).

Corfu Town features one-off shops such as **Souzos** (42 Guilford Street), where the family's heritage of handmade furniture goes back more than a century, as well as the **Patounis soap factory** on San Rocco Square which crafts soaps from olive oil.

THIS PAGE (FROM TOP): Natural food products such as mastic resin have never lost their appeal in Greece; ouzo is a staple in many local bars; Cretan carpets are created on looms in a village on the Lasithi Plateau.

OPPOSITE: Reproduced religious icons are displayed for sale in the Meteora region of central Greece.

epicurean greece

With Greek expatriates spread far and wide around the globe and many cities flaunting their own Hellenic eateries, Greek cuisine is cherished by people who have never even set foot in the country. It also helps that Greek food is light, fresh and healthy.

'We are lovers of the beautiful, yet simple in our tastes,' wrote the vaunted historian Thucydides. While he may have been referring to Greek culture in general, the phrase is especially apt when it comes to Greek food. Although there are plenty of complicated dishes and recipes, the beauty of Greek food lies mainly in its simplicity. The countryside is flush with herbs, nuts and fruits; ingredients as simple as goat cheese and Kalamata olives—without any sort of garnish other than a light sprinkling of oregano and olive oil—can transform into a gourmet meal when combined with a bottle of fine local wine and a spectacular setting.

Like most Mediterranean cooking, the key to Greek fare is fresh ingredients from the sea, gardens and fields. A mature olive tree, a tomato and cucumber patch, and a couple of sheep or goats are really all one needs to create the basic ingredients of many a Greek dish. Cooking methods tend to be simple: roast it on the spit, bake it in the oven, and in the case of vegetables, simply serve them uncooked with a sprinkling of herbs and olive oil. Although the sunny Mediterranean climate may look homogeneous to outsiders, there are subtle changes from season to season, which in turn affect the ingredients that go into the dishes.

Greek cuisine traces its roots back several thousand years, although—truth be told—the ancient Greeks would be hard-pressed to recognise anything in a modern restaurant. Some dishes, such as *skordalia*, a garlic and potato purée, do endure however.

While many basic ingredients remain the same, centuries of outside influence—from the Romans, Byzantines and Ottomans, in particular—have transformed native cuisine into something far different from the food eaten during the age of Aristotle and Alexander. As a matter of fact, contemporary Greek dishes actually has much more in common with Turkish cuisine.

culinary talents

'Greek food has not assumed its rightful place on the world's gastronomical map,' says celebrity chef Yiannis Baxevanis. That gap is quickly closing, thanks to the efforts of Baxevanis and other top chefs who are hoisting the flag of Greek cooking both at home and abroad.

Baxevanis is typical of a new wave of young chefs who have combined Greek ingredients with French methods and American marketing panache, creating nouvelle Greek cuisine and restaurants like nothing Greece has ever seen before.

Athens-born-and-bred, he trained for five years in France before returning to his homeland, where he directed the kitchens at the Mykonos Blu resort on Mykonos and the Lagonissi resort near Cape Sounion in Attica, as well as his own restaurant, **Giorti Baxevanis**, in the Athens suburb of Chaidari (Iera Odos Avenue). He has also recently launched trendy Greek eateries in New York City and Dubai.

Another culinary star is Lefteris Lazarou, founder of **Varoulko** (80 Piraeus Street) in Athens, one of the few restaurants in Greece to earn a Michelin star. Son of a seagoing cook and raised in the gritty old port of Piraeus, Lazarou parlayed everything he learned as a child into the capital's top seafood spot. He was also in charge of Greek cuisine for the Athens 2004 Olympic committee.

Other star chefs include Istanbul-born dessert maestro and cookbook author Stelios Parliaros, and Cypriot Christoforos Peskias, whose flavourful cretan dishes at **Dakos** (6 Tsakalof Street, Kolonaki) continue to enthrall gourmands.

Further afield is **Domata** (Sani Resort, Kassandra, Chalkidiki) where Chrysanthos Karamolekos' new Greek cuisine constantly surprises even the most seasoned of palettes.

Ettore Botrini (of Frame Bar fame) also has another gastronomical hit under his belt: **Etrusco** (Kato, Korakiana, Corfu) is indeed a coveted treat with scrumptious Italian creations made from fresh ingredients.

iconic dishes

One could easily make a whole meal from a typical Greek salad (olives, onions, tomatoes, cucumber and *feta* cheese in an olive oil dressing) or celebrated *meze* appetisers such as *taramosalata* (puréed fish roe with olive oil, lemon juice and day-old bread), *dolmades* (stuffed grapevine leaves), *spanakopita* (phyllo pastry filled with spinach and *feta* cheese), and *tzatziki* (a mix of plain yoghurt, garlic and diced cucumber).

Among the more familiar entrées are traditional standards such as *souvlaki* (marinated meat grilled on a skewer), *gyros* (meat roasted on a vertical spit) and *moussaka* (a baked dish normally made with eggplant, minced meat and a béchamel topping).

Other luscious creations include *Kleftiko* is lamb meat marinated in garlic and lemon juice and slow-baked in an oven or open pit to the point where it almost melts in the mouth. The name translates directly to mean 'the thief', and is attributed to the sheep rustlers in the old days who cooked their stolen animals underground to avoid detection. *Pastitzio* is the Greek version of lasagne: layers of tubular pasta, cheese, tomato and ground meat, covered in *béchamel* sauce.

There are also a number of native vegetarian dishes such as *yemista* (baked stuffed peppers or tomatoes), *prassorizo* (leek risotto), and *briám* (mixed vegetables cooked in tomato sauce).

Local soups include *revithia* (chick pea or garbanzo bean soup) and the hearty *psarosoupa* (fish soup with rice or potatoes, vegetables, lemon juice and olive oil).

Bread is considered nearly sacred in Greek cuisine, especially the omnipresent *pita*, which can be eaten plain or with traditional Greek *mezes* such as *taramosalata* or *tzatziki*. Other varieties of Greek bread include black olive bread, honey and walnut croissants, and *tsourekia* (braided

THIS PAGE (FROM TOP): *Watermelon, Kalamata olives and feta cheese come together to produce a refreshing Greek summer treat; the Galaxy Roof Restaurant of the Hilton Athens hotel offers al fresco dining and unhindered city views.*

OPPOSITE: *The menu isn't the only thing that draws the eye in Meat Me restaurant at the Classical BabyGrand Hotel in Athens.*

Easter rolls). There are also dozens of types of cheese, which can be made from goat, sheep and cow's milk. Foremost is the world-famous *feta. Anthotyros*, which translates to 'flower cheese'—so named for its delicate floral taste—is a soft and creamy cheese which, when aged, becomes the dry and highly aromatic *myzithra*. Other prized cheeses include smoked *metsovone* and the hard, slightly salty *kefalotyri*.

There are thousands of traditional restaurants all over Greece. Some of the finest can be found in the Plaka district of central Athens, at the foot of the Acropolis. One can dine well with contemporary yet sumptuous Greek cuisine at **Kuzina** (9 Adrianou Steet) and **To Kouti** (23 Adrianou Street), or try the traditional dishes at **O Platanos** (4 Diogenous Street, Plaka), **Vlassis** (8 Paster Street) and **Dioskouri** (16 D. Vasiliou Street).

Going even further back, **Archaion Gefsis**, translated to mean 'Ancient Flavours', specialises in popular dishes from classical Greece such as *epiplous* (fried liver wrapped in lamb accompanied by asparagus, eggs and cheese) and *creokakkabos* (pork pancetta with sweet and sour sauce made from honey, thyme, vinegar and chickpeas).

regional treats

Although many of the more popular dishes are found throughout the nation, Greece's various regions have their own culinary specialities.

On the huge island of Crete, the food tends to be spicier than on the mainland. There are myriad local treats ranging from *kotopoulo pilafi* (chicken pilaf) to *choirinó kritikó* (pork cutlets). Even within Crete, there are regional specialities, such as *haniotiko boureki*—a baked blend of potato, zucchini, cheese and mint from the Chania district of western Crete.

Along the white sands of Elounda, **Kafenion** and **Dionyssos** (Elounda Beach, Crete) both serve sumptuous Cretan and Greek cuisine with exceptional wine menus that have received five-star diamond recognition from publications such as *Wine Spectator*, while **Thalassa** (Elounda Bay, Crete) offers a lush variety of grilled fresh fish and regional seafood specialities.

For those who can't get transportation to the villages, Iraklion has a number of restaurants that serve traditional Greek and Cretan dishes. Lodged inside a whitewashed house, **Erganos Taverna** (5 Georgiadi Street) specialises in *sarikopites* pies stuffed with honey, cheese and wild herbs; savour them accompanied by the strains of local *mandinades* music.

Kiriakos (53 Dimokratias Street) has been an island dining institution for over three decades. It is an elegant bistro where the menu includes Cretan-style casseroles, calamari in *ouzo* and basil, rooster in a red wine sauce, and baked aubergines stuffed with veal.

The speciality in Corfu is a hearty vegetable and pasta soup called *bourou-bourou*, which has been around since Venetian days. Given its eclectic history—and the various empires that controlled it prior to the 20th century—the Ionian isles boasts the country's most distinct regional cuisine. The best place to taste it is in the old part of Corfu Town, with its cobblestone squares and ancient stone walls.

In Corfu Town, the **Venetian Well** (Kremasti Square) is tucked between an old church and the 17th-century water well from which the restaurant takes its name. Its menu blends Greek, Italian and Balkan influences. The family-run **Aegli Garden Restaurant** (23 Kapodistriou Street), located in the romantic Listón arcade, offers a number of Corfiote delicacies, including *pastitsada* (baked veal and pasta casserole).

Central Greece is blessed with all sorts of culinary hybrids and crossovers. *Pittes* are savoury pies stuffed with meat, cheese and vegetables, popular in the Epirus region. *Spetsofai*, a hot pot made with spicy country sausage, bell peppers, onions, garlic and wine, hails from the Pelion region. Freshwater fish is another speciality of central Greece.

The lakeside city of Ioánnina offers a number of eateries with waterfront views and interesting local cuisine. Among the dishes of **I Prasini Akti** (The Green Coast) are lake fish, crabs and eel. The Pelion and adjacent Sporades regions have emerged as culinary hubs, with places such as **Dryades** restaurant (Dryades Hotel), in the romantic village of Agios Lavrentios, drawing much attention. The port city of Volos boasts more than 350 *tsipouradiko*—café-bars that specialise in *tsipouro* and traditional Greek *meze* appetisers, including various regional treats. They tend to concentrate along the waterfront and the time-

worn Nea Ionia neighbourhood. In establishments such as **Bokos** (143 Maiandrou Street, Volos), old Greece still seems very much alive.

Heavily influenced by Balkan and Turkish culinary traditions and generally more Middle Eastern in character, Macedonian cuisine is often akin to dining in another country altogether. The cuisine up north also favours seafood (cuttlefish and mussels in particular) and zesty dishes such as *soutzoukákia* (meatballs with rice and tomato sauce). Northern Greece features an increasingly chic regional dining scene, especially in the renaissance city of Thessaloniki.

Here, warehouses in the old Ladadika neighbourhood, which were once used to store olive oil, have morphed into gourmet eateries such as **Zithos** (5 Katouni Street), with its spicy Middle Eastern-style grills, fresh seafood and salads. Gourmands yearning for savoury *mezes* or freshly grilled fish will not be disappointed with **Ouzaki** (58 Psilantou Street), **Aristotelis** (8 Aristotelous Street) or **Mavri Thalassa** (63 An. Thrakis Street).

The ambience is even more exotic in the town of Kavala, where the **Imaret** restaurant (30–32 Theodorou Poulidou Street) lies within the domed confines of early 19th-century Ottoman buildings; diners dine on the outdoor terrace overlooking the harbour or in the elegant candlelit dining room.

international eats

The absorption of Greece into the European Union, combined with half a century of tourism and an increasing number of Greeks who

travel abroad, has generated a taste for global food—cravings that are satisfied by a growing number of international eateries. As with almost all other trends, Athens leads the way, especially in the trendy inner city neighbourhoods of Psirri and Kolonaki. They are the first stops for adventurous gourmands in search of new and unusual treats.

On any given night, one can metaphorically dine one's way around the globe on the streets of Athens. At the ultra-posh **Spondi** (5 Pyrronos Street, Pagrati), the menu runs all the way from venison in a Sarawak-style pepper sauce and lobster *maki* rolls, to partridge with *foie gras* and rabbit soup. Thirteen types of shellfish are served at the medieval English-themed **Avalon** (20 Leokoriou Street, Psirri).

African and Middle Eastern dishes are the speciality at **Hilies Kai Dyo Nihtes** (10 Karaeskaki Street, Psirri), where the after-dinner entertainment includes belly dancers. **Cubanita Habana** (28 Karaeskaki Street, Psirri) offers live Latin music and spicy Caribbean cuisine in equal measures, while cosy **Freudian Oriental** (21 Xenokratous Street, Kolonaki), and the edgy **Matsuhisa Athens** (40 Apollonos Street, Vouliagmeni) will impress with their contemporary Japanese fare.

Other choices for international fare in Athens include the trendy **Meat Me Restaurant** at the Classical BabyGrand Hotel, which offers huge juicy burgers; **Milos Restaurant** (Hilton Athens), helmed by the celebrated Costas Spiliadis of Milos New York fame; and **Galaxy Bar** (Hilton Athens), .where patrons dine under the stars.

Fusion cuisine takes centrestage at **Island Club & Restaurant** (27th km of Athens-Sounion Avenue) and **Central** (14 Kolonaki Square), where executive chef Nikos Skliras reveals his culinary talent via innovative Greek-Asian creations. Wine connoisseurs can savour contemporary Italian cuisine alongside an excellent wine menu at **Wine Gallery** (Athens Life Gallery), while the Grand Resort Lagonissi's **Veghera Club Restaurant** combines mouth-watering dishes with stunning sea views.

Given their cosmopolitan nature, the islands are also blessed with incredible international cuisines, as exemplified by Japanese fusion delicacies at **Matsuhisa Mykonos** (Hotel Belvedere) and the savoury Thai fish cakes and chicken satay at **Blue Ginger** (Argyraina) on Mykonos.

Perched on the edge of a volcanic caldera in Santorini is the delectable **Selene** restaurant (Fira), with its creative repertoire of international fusion dishes.

Blue Lagoon (Elounda Beach, Crete) offers sumptuous Polynesian cuisine and a sushi bar, while

La Bouillabaisse (Minos Beach Art Hotel) will tantalise the tastebuds with its French *haute cuisine*.

kombolói society

Like other Mediterranean civilisations, local life revolves around communal dining, primarily at cafés set beneath grapevine trellises or around boat-filled harbours. People gossiping about their neighbours; widows clad in black; old men methodically fingering their *kombolói* beads (Greek worry beads) as a form of relaxation—all set against a backdrop of noise and wonderful aromas from the kitchen.

A cultural and psychological extension of the worry beads after which it is named, *kombolói* society is the Greek equivalent of the café society that thrives in the Mediterranean, with an attitude that life's too short to rush through. This laidback lifestyle was once considered an anachronism, not in keeping with the industrial and commercial powerhouse that Greece longed to become.

Having caught up with the rest of the Western world, however, many Greeks have come to embrace *kombolói* society as an essential part of their being. While their accoutrements may have been updated (mobile phones rather than newspapers, iPods rather than radios)—the basic message is the same: take time to stop and smell the roses.

In villages and older urban areas, residents would put aside time to gather at the local *estiatórion* or taverna. The former is best described as a neighbourhood restaurant where local dishes and drinks are served throughout the day; the latter are bars that also serve food, generally open from early evening until after midnight. Other varieties include an *ouzeri*, a tavern that specialises in *ouzo* and *meze* dishes, while the *kafeneía* is a neighbourhood coffee bar.

Greek coffee is strong, dark and traditionally brewed in a small copper pot (*briki*). Freshly ground coffee is brewed over medium heat, with constant stirring until the grounds have dissolved. The finished product should have thick foam on top and grounds at the bottom, and is served in *demitasse* cups. Sugar is added during the brewing process and determines the type of coffee—*sketos* is coffee without sugar, *metrios* has just a dash of sugar, *glykos* is normally two teaspoons while *vary glykos* is the strongest in terms of both caffeine content and sugar.

Greeks take their coffee with a cold glass of water and without ice. Cookies, biscuits and *loukoumia* (a Greek version of Turkish delight made from almonds, honey and rose water) are common accompaniments. The *frappé*—iced coffee topped with thick foam—was invented in Greece in the 1950s and spread around the world as a popular hot-weather drink.

Coffee connoisseurs can savour well-blended brews—Greek or Italian style—and pastries along the many cafés along Kolonaki Square. The *fin-de-siecle* interior of **Zonar's** (Panapistimiou and Voukourestiou streets) transforms coffee drinking into a grand experience, while patisserie **Hatzis** (5 Metropoleos Street) will satiate the sweet tooth with delicate Greek confectionery.

THIS PAGE (FROM TOP): Traditional tavernas line a street in Nafplion, one of the culinary hubs of the Peloponnese region; some of the creations at Spondi could easily double as works of art.

OPPOSITE (FROM TOP): Dining at Matsuhisa Mykonos in Hotel Belvedere is all the rage; Grand Resort Lagonissi hotel offers fine dining and sumptuous views on the Attica coast near Athens.

greek libations

'Where there is no wine, there is no love,' wrote Euripides in the 5th century BC. And indeed, the Greeks have always loved their wine. They've been making it longer than just about anyone else on the planet and they once had the audacity to elevate the mashing and fermentation of grapes—as well as the imbibing of the final product—to a mystical level through the cult of Dionysus, the blissful god of Greek wine.

But the story of Greek wine is also one of rebirth and reversal of fortune. Relegated to second-class status by the rise of French, German and later Californian and Australian wineries, the industry languished for decades and Greece nearly lost the art of winemaking. It was only in the last 30 years that a whole new generation of vintners has revived the golden days, producing not just the finer wines in the eastern Mediterranean, but also some of the best appellations in the entire world.

origins + ancient wines

Recent digs at a Neolithic site at Dikili Tash in eastern Macedonia revealed evidence of winemaking as early as 4500 BC. By the second millennium BC, Greek wine stored in amphorae was one of the premium products of Mediterranean trade; Greeks were actively spreading viniculture by introducing grape cultivation and fermentation to their colonies in Spain, Italy and southern France.

References to wine are found throughout ancient Greek prose. 'Nothing more excellent nor more valuable than wine was ever granted mankind by God,' wrote Plato. The historian Thucydides claimed that the peoples of the Mediterranean finally emerged from barbarism only 'when they learnt to cultivate the olive and the vine.' Wine was one of Homer's favourite topics, the source of any number of memorable quips such as 'Bacchus [Dionysus] opens the gate of the heart.' Hippocrates was known to prescribe wine for medicinal purposes and wine was a popular topic at symposia, during which participants would eat, drink and discuss philosophical subjects.

The Crusaders picked up right where the ancients left off, cultivating grapes and mashing them into wine on the islands between the Greek mainland and the Holy Land.

Commandaria, the world's oldest continuous appellation, was originally bottled by the Knights Templar on what was then the Greek island of Cyprus. Greek wine was also immensely popular with the crowned heads of Europe, featuring at Richard the Lion Hearted's wedding. Literature and trade records from the Middle Ages also mention a number of Greek wines, commonly known then as Malmsey and Rumney, both cultivated from the southern Peloponnese.

Winemaking continued in Ottoman times and the early years of Greek independence. But due to various social and economic reasons (including warfare, emigration and natural disasters), Hellenic winemaking fell into a century-long period of decline and neglect.

revival + renaissance

The Ministry of Agriculture attempted to jump start the wine industry in 1937 with the establishment of a National Wine Institute. And it might have succeeded but for the fact that WW II began just a few years later. As a result, the revival of Greek winemaking was delayed until the 1950s, when modern viniculture was introduced for the first time.

In the wake of private investment in the very latest winemaking technology and the adoption of sophisticated modern marketing techniques, the Greek wine industry has undergone a tremendous upsurge in recent decades. A new generation of native winemakers—**Evangelos Gerovassiliou, Vassilis Tsaktsarlis** and **Angelos Iatridis** to name a few—has trained in viniculture and oenology at world-renowned institutions such as the Ecole du Vin in Bordeaux and the University of California.

Ambitious as they are clever, many new-wave winemakers such as **Stellios Boutaris** reinforced their agricultural studies with management degrees from the likes of Harvard and INSEAD.

Greece's entry into the European Union in 1981 suddenly opened the doors to a much larger market for Greek wine. The industry got yet another financial boost when Greece finally switched from the drachma to the euro in 2001. Since then, history, technology and education have converged to develop distinctive wines that are attaining worldwide acclaim and receiving the highest awards at international competitions.

two hundred and fifty varieties

The uniqueness of Greek wine stems from the fact that there are 250 local varieties of grapes. Of the 250, 45 varieties are used in modern winemaking as well as mixed with international grape varieties to produce other distinctive blends. This variety combined with pervading sunshine, low rainfall and the country's fertile lands provide first-rate criteria for wine production.

Perhaps the best known of the native grapes is the lusciously dark Xinomavro, a favourite of the Macedonian vineyards and the soul of many an excellent red wine. The name translates into the frightful sounding 'Sour Black' but there's nothing the least bit ominous about the grape's outstanding quality, often compared to the California Pinot Noir or Burgundy reds.

Other top-notch reds are the fruity Agiorghitiko ('St George') grown throughout Greece, the Mandelaria of the Aegean islands, and the melodious Mavrodaphne ('Black Daphne') of the Ionian islands and the nearby northern Peloponnese, which is often blended with Korinthiaki grapes to produce the sweet, fortified dessert wine of the same name.

Greece boasts almost 20 varieties of grapes used in the creation of its white wines. Known for its citrus overtones and delicate notes, Roditis is a grape that is popular throughout Greece, with the finer wines derived from grapes grown in vineyards on Patras' rugged slopes in the Peloponnese.

THIS PAGE (ANTICLOCKWISE FROM TOP): 4th-century wine blending vessels in the New Acropolis Museum reflect Greece's long and rich viniculture heritage; a bust of Dionysus, the ancient Greek god of wine; Roman-era coins decorated with vine leaves and Greek writing.

OPPOSITE: A small hillside vineyard near Manolates village on Samos island in the northern Aegean.

Although also found throughout the country, Assyrtiko grapes are associated with the Aegean islands, in particular Santorini, where it yields an elegant dry while with citrus overtones and an earthy aftertaste attributed to Santorini's volcanic soul. Another celebrated white cultivar is Malagousia, nearly extinct until it was suddenly revived in the 1980s by Macedonia's **Domaine Gerovassiliou**.

major wine regions

The main regions for grape cultivation are located in the Ionian islands, Macedonia, central Greece and the Peloponnese. Macedonia in particular has gained a reputation for producing superior wines, thanks to the likes of cutting-edge vineyards like **Ktima Kir Yianni** (near Yianakohori), **Ktima Biblia Chora** (just west of Kavala) and **Alpha Estate** (near Florina). The homeland of Alexander the Great boasts several distinct appellation (AOC) regions, none more famous than Naoussa and the nearby Amyndeon plateau, where Xinomavro grapes are transformed into marvellous red vintages and rosés known especially for their continental flavour.

Most of the grapes grown in central Greece come from the southeast corner of Continental Greece, between Athens and Lamia, where many of the vineyards thrive in the shadow of snowcapped Mount Parnassus. **Estate Hatzimichalis** (near Atalanti) has already emerged as a quality vintner in recent years, with a stellar reputation that extends beyond Grecian shores. The area is also the homeland of *retsina*, the dry white wine with a hint of pine resin.

With diverse geography and microclimates, the Peloponnese turns out a wide variety of wines, none better than those found at **GAIA Estate** (Nemea), Angelos Rouvalis' **Oenoforos** (Selinous, 25 100 Aigio) and **A.S. Parparoussis** (1 Achilleos Street, 264 42 Proastio Patron) where the blend of native Agiorghitiko and Cabernet Sauvignon grapes has produced incredible vintages. The peninsula now accounts for around 25 percent of Greek wine production and includes the celebrated reds of Nemea, and the whites of Pátras and Mantinia.

Major wine-producing islands include Crete, Mykonos and Santorini in the Aegean, and Cephalonia in the Ionian Sea over on the western flank of Greece. With an ideal climate and soil for growing superior grapes, Crete alone accounts for producing about 20 percent of all Greek wines. The huge island is also home to the oldest winery ever discovered—an ancient press at Archanes that dates back to the Minoan age. **Douloufakis** (near Dafnes) is one of the older and more prestigious Cretan wineries. Founded in 1930, the winery is still a family business after all these years.

The Aegean isles also have a long history of wine production and were integral to the migration of viticulture across the Mediterranean in olden times.

wine institute appellations

In the early 1970s, the Wine Institute established appellation laws similar to the rest of Europe which divided Greek wine into four broad categories: OPE, OPAP, local wines and table wines. Appellation laws are now administered by a branch of the Ministry of Agriculture called KEPO (Central Committee for the Protection of Wine Production). Other than aging, factors that help to determine qualifying products and areas include the historic pedigree of the grape; elevation, orientation, soil and yield of the vineyard; and the type of aging process.

OPE (Onomasía Proeléfseos Eleghoméni) is a controlled appellation of origin, the Greek equivalent to the French VQPRD. Only a handful of Greek wines qualify for this category—all of them are sweet—and this include the muscat wines of Limnos, Rhodes, Patras, Samos, Cephalonia and Mavrodaphni. OPE is identified by a blue banderole over the bottle's mouth.

OPAP (Onomasía Proeléfseos Anotéras Piótitos) are appellations of origin of superior quality, the local equivalent of the French VLQPRD. The group currently includes about 25 red and white wines, distinguished by a red banderole over the bottle's mouth. The appellations are scattered throughout the nation: Amynteo and Naoussa in Macedonia; Patras, Mantinia and Nemea in the Peloponnese; Robola of Cephalonia; and four different appellations on Crete.

Around 140 wines are designated as *Topikos Inos*, equivalent to the French *vins de pays*. There are also table wines—*Epitrapezios Inos*—a category similar to the French *vins de table*.

Additionally, producers of OPE and OPAP are allowed to use the word 'Reserve' on white wines that have been aged for two years and red wines aged for three years. The term 'Grand Reserve' can be used on white wines aged for a minimum of three years and red wines a minimum of four years.

other grape-based drinks

Before the resurgence of the wine industry, other grape-based drinks led the charge in Greece.

Metaxa is a twice-distilled brandy aged in oak barrels and blended with muscat wine and botanical herbs. Generally *metaxa* is sold as three-, five- or seven-star, with the stars representing the number of years it has been aged in casks. There is also a Metaxa Private Reserve, aged for at least two decades.

Tsipouro is a distilled spirit made from the 'pomace' residue of the wine press. It boasts a long history, dating back to the 14th century and the *tsipouro*-making monks on Mount Athos. Drunk hot or cold, it contains 45 percent alcohol by volume and is usually served in shot glasses. It's mostly made in Thessaly, Epirus and Macedonia, where an anise-flavoured variety is sold as well. A stronger version is *tsikoudia* or *raki*, frequently served as a digestif in restaurants.

Retsina is even older, with roots that go back 2,000 to 3,000 years. Modern researchers think the resin-scented drink originally came about by accident, from the olden-day habit of sealing wine amphora with pine resin to aid in preservation.

The pine aroma became so popular that today, *retsina* is infused with small pieces of pine resin during the winemaking process. Nowadays it's produced all over Greece but the best is thought to come from Attica, Boeotia and Euboea.

THIS PAGE (FROM TOP): Music and wine blend easily at Ktima Biblia Chora on the slopes of Mount Pangeon; a sommelier serves wine at a trendy restaurant in Athens; skilled hands have been harvesting Greek grapes all over the country for nearly seven millennia.
OPPOSITE: A private tasting room at the upscale Domaine Gerovassiliou winery in Macedonia.

greece after dark

With the wine-adoring Dionysus as one of their most beloved gods, the ancient Greeks certainly knew a thing or two about entertaining themselves. But the excesses of the ancients pales in comparison to Greece's eclectic modern nightlife.

One expects a city with five million souls to have an awesome nightlife, and Athens certainly doesn't miss a beat. The dilemma comes from having too much choice—there are literally hundreds of places to dress up for and one can paint the town red on any given night.

Fans of modern opera, ballet and orchestral music will delight in the programmes offered at the **Megaron Mousikis concert hall** (Vassilissis Sofias Avenue and Kokkali Street) as well as **The Greek National Opera,** (59-61 Academias Street), soon to have a new odeon and opera house designed by the renown architect Renzo Piano.

The imposing **National Theatre of Greece** (22 Aghiou Konstantinou Street) presents a broad array of European, American and Greek theatre, ranging from Shakespeare to rebellious 'anti-opera'. During the summer months, classical music and drama are staged in the timeless setting of the **Herodes Atticus Amphitheatre** on the south side of the Acropolis with some of the finest acoustics in the world thanks to its ancient yet superb architectural design and marble construction. Much of the annual **Athens Festival** takes place on this open-air stage, with the façade of the Parthenon looming over 5,000 spectators.

Many of the restaurants and clubs of the old **Plaka district** feature traditional Greek folk music performed on accordion and *bouzouki* mandolin. Known for its live music sessions and *rembetika* singers, **Abyssinia Cafe** (Plateia Abyssinias) is centrally located in Monastiraki.

The capital's young, hip nightlife scene revolves around Kolonaki, Exarchia, Psirri and Gazi—all of them with distinct personalities. The swish **Kolonaki** district is the place to go for coffee and cocktails as the sun sets. The design-savvy **Frame Lounge Bar** (1 Deinokratous Street) is typical of the area, a place where local hipsters come to see and be seen.

Exarchia is the Athens version of New York's Greenwich Village, a heady mélange of cafés and clubs where students and artists mingle. In that same vein, **An Club** (13–15 Solomou Street) is a long-standing rock club that hosts the best touring European bands while **Rempétiki Istoria** (181 Ippokratous Street), the oldest *rembetika* club in Athens, is an institution renowned for its authentic folk music.

Situated between City Hall and the Keramikos Cemetery, **Psirri** boasts more clubbing venues than any other part of Athens. Among the pillars of the local music establishment are **Aristofanis** (Taki Street), **House of Art** (4 Saktouri Street), **Cubanita Habana Club** (28 Karaeskaki Street) and **Hytra** (7 Navarxou Apostoli Street).

Just off Pireos Street, **Gazi** is home to trendy venues such as the kindergarten-turned-nightclub **Nipiagogeio** (Elasidon and Kleanthous streets) or the hip **Mamacas** bar and restaurant (41 Persephone Street).

Greek islands are also renowned for their nightlife, in particular Mykonos, Corfu, Santorini and Rhodes. All of them have Ibiza-style dance clubs where house, break beats and trance dominate the turntable, often spun by guest DJs from London, New York Amsterdam and other party capitals.

The most glamourous bash on **Mykonos** has got to be the annual White Party held at the **Hotel Belvedere**, complete with world-famous DJs, international celebrities and an all-white dress code. **Santorini**'s top hangout is **Koo Club** in Fira while **Rhodes** gives visitors the option of lounging ala 'James Bond' at **Casino Rodos** (4 G Papanikolaou Street).

Thessaloniki's nightlife revolves around **Plateia Aristotélous**' waterfront with its outdoor cafés, and the funky **Ladadika** district where **Mylos**, a coverted flour mill, seamlessly blends art, comedy and music together.

As a thriving university town and port, **Patras** also has an edgy nightlife vibe, especially during the carnival and summer months when the streets rock to live music into the wee hours of the morning. **Riga Ferreao, Aghios Nikolaos** and **Radinou Streets** in the central city are flanked by stylish designer clubs and bars. The music ranges from funky world beats at **Notos** (80 Patreos Street), to live *bouzouki* at **Harama** (Mezonos and Kapodistriou streets), and sexy lounge sounds at **Distinto Espresso Bar** (King George Square).

THIS PAGE (FROM TOP): Dance events on Mykonos draw hipsters from all around the globe; pop art decorates a club in the trendy Psirri district of Athens; Greek bars are known for their wide range of locally made liqueurs.

OPPOSITE (FROM TOP): Greek singing legend Nana Mouskouri performs at Herodes Atticus Amphitheatre; a bouzouki player at one of the traditional tavernas in Athens.

yachting: an odyssey

With hundreds of islands and countless coves and bays, Greece is a paradise for anyone who craves holidays at sea. An aquamarine playground for the rich and famous even in the 1960s, the Aegean Sea still remains a yachting hub for celebrity sailing.

Tom Hanks and his Greek-American wife Rita Wilson, as well as fellow Hollywood icon Brad Pitt, are known to frequent the waters around Antiparos in the Cyclades. The late Greek power couple Ari and Jackie O were also known to flit back and forth between Mykonos and Corfu. But given the celebrity penchant for privacy, one is more likely to run into their boats in the most remote places around Greece.

The country also has its fair share of ordinary sailors, folks who charter boats, sign up for guided flotilla trips, or sail their own boat from some obscure home port to fulfill a lifetime dream to sail the Greek isles.

Due to the short distances between islands and safe sailing conditions, Greece provides ideal yachting conditions throughout the year. Summer can be crowded and rather hot, so plan a cruise outside of the peak months. Spring and autumn make memorable sailing trips, but even winter can be delightful.

Some areas are more conducive to island-hopping than others, in particular the small and intimate **Sporades** in the northern Aegean. Only five of the 24 islands are inhabited, with none of them more than a few hours' sail from one another.

The **Dodecanese** between Rhodes and Samos are another sailing paradise, a chain of closely spaced islands along the Turkish coast with loads of coves, charming ports and calm sea crossings between each island.

Those who want to combine their sailing with underwater adventure should head for **Chios Island**, named one of the '100 best dive sites in the world' by Britain's *Scuba Travel* magazine. Among the island's submarine attractions are submerged caves, myriads of fish and small shipwrecks. Other top dive spots include **Santorini**, **Lefkas**, **Tzia** and the waters off **Elounda Bay** on **Crete**.

As the nation's oldest yachting centre, the port of **Pireaus** also houses the lion's share of prestigious yacht clubs, none more so than the chic **Yacht Club of Greece** (18 Karageorgi Servias Street, Pireaus). Founded in 1933 by a group of prominent Athenians, the club gained royal patronage 40 years later when King George II accepted the title of Admiral of the Club. Today, the club boasts 1,550 members which include many Athens-based diplomats and leading naval officers.

Another celebrated sailing haven is the **Hellenic Offshore Racing Club** (3 Akti Athinas Dilaveri, Pireaus), which promotes competitive sailing throughout Greece.

Greece has about 16,000 km (9,942 miles) of coastland offering a rich diversity of white- and black-sand beaches, pebbly coves, hidden sea caves and sheer cliffs. Touring by boat allows visitors to experience Greece at their own pace and visit picturesque ports, seaside villages and secluded bays— almost impossible to experience if one only travels by land.

Chartering a yacht upon reaching Greece is another option, especially one-way charters that offer sailors the opportunity of not having to backtrack to the original port when the cruise is over.

Hellenic Charters (Aristofanous Street, Glyfada) offers an incredible range of luxury sailing choices from do-it-yourself bareboat charters to fully crewed and stocked boats, to flotilla programmes for family sailing fun. Their fleet includes large and smaller luxury motor yachts, catamarans and monohull sailboats. But the queen of the fleet has to be the revamped *Christina*, the gigantic Onassis WW II warship-turned-luxury-yacht and host to countless celebrities from Winston Churchill and Eva Peron to Greta Garbo, Frank Sinatra and Elizabeth Taylor. The price tag? A cool US$86,000 per day including 36 crew.

Global yacht charter company **The Moorings** offers six charter locations in Greece—**Athens**, **Corfu**, **Kos**, **Lefkas**, **Skiathos** and **Syros**. Their modern monohulls and catamarans accommodate two to ten passengers in the utmost comfort. Charters can be completely bareboat, fully crewed or staffed with just a moorings skipper and/or cook.

eYachtCharter.com is an Internet-based directory of yachts for charters worldwide. At any given time it offers approximately a dozen luxury boats for charter out of Athens, Piraeus and the Ionian Islands (from bareboat to including skipper and cook) as well as the *Nima Star II* motor yacht which comes fully crewed and sleeps up to eight passengers.

Fully organised group sailing trips are an alternative option. **National Geographic Expeditions**, in association with **Lindblad Expeditions**, offers family trips through **the Cyclades** aboard the sail-assisted motor yacht *SV Panorama*. With intimate, comfortable cabins and well-appointed public areas, the 41-passenger vessel mixes stunning antiquities and boutique shopping with swimming and snorkelling.

Smithsonian Journeys offers cruises aboard the tall ship *Sea Cloud* to ancient sites and quaint little ports around the Aegean Sea. The four-masted vessels offers an old-fashioned sailing experience as well as the luxury and romance of a bygone era. Cruising from Istanbul to Athens, passengers explore the art, culture and history of ancient sites such as **Pergamon**, **Ephesus** and **Santorini**. Throughout the journey, a classical archaeologist provides a richer understanding of Aegean cultures.

THIS PAGE *(FROM TOP): Regatta tours are an increasingly popular way to explore the Greek isles; those with enough experience can charter their own bareboat yacht from several outfits in Greece; a local fishing harbour doubles up as a 'marina' for visiting yachtsmen.*
OPPOSITE: *With its deserted beach and submerged wreck, secluded Smuggler's Cove on Zakynthos is an ideal place to drop anchor.*

athens+greaterattica

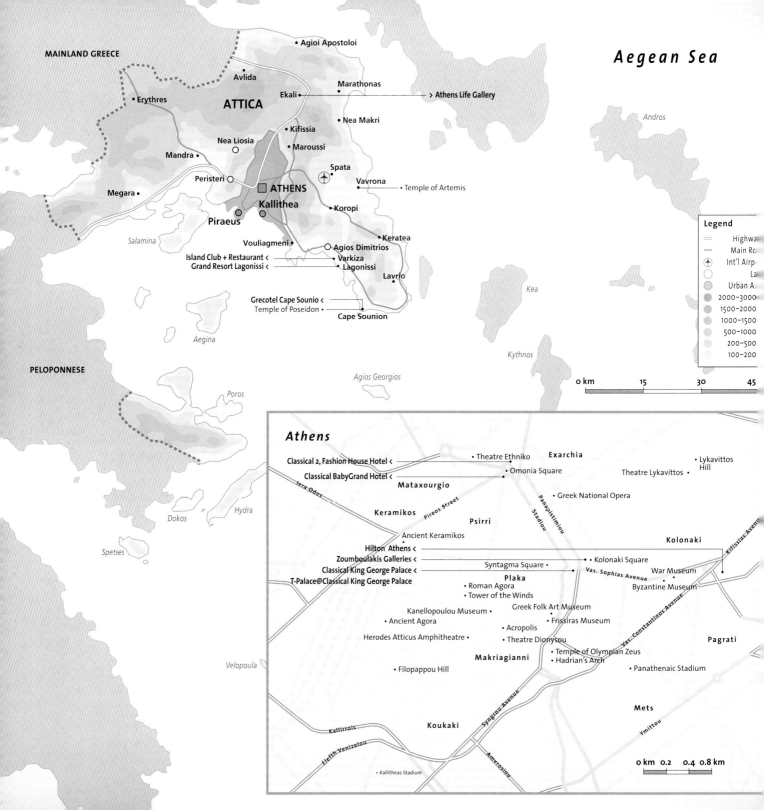

MAINLAND GREECE

Aegean Sea

• Agioi Apostoloi

• Avlida

ATTICA

Ekali •
Marathonas • ──────────── > Athens Life Gallery

• Erythres

• Kifissia

• Nea Makri

Nea Liosia ○

Mandra •

• Maroussi

Peristeri ○

Spata
✈

ATHENS

Vavrona • ── • Temple of Artemis

Kallithea ○

• Koropi

Piraeus ○

Megara •

Salamina

• Keratea

Vouliagmeni •

Agios Dimitrios ○

Island Club + Restaurant < ──────── • Varkiza
Grand Resort Lagonissi < ──────── • Lagonissi

• Lavrio

Grecotel Cape Sounio <
Temple of Poseidon • ──── • Cape Sounion

Aegina

Andros

Kea

PELOPONNESE

Poros

Kythnos

Agios Georgios

Dokos *Hydra*

Spetses

Velopoula

Athens

Classical 2, Fashion House Hotel < ──────── • Theatre Ethniko   **Exarchia**

Classical BabyGrand Hotel < ──────── • Omonia Square

Mataxourgio

Iera Odos

Keramikos   *Pireos Street*   **Psirri**

Ancient Keramikos •

Hilton Athens < ─────────────────────────
Zoumboulakis Galleries < ────────────
Classical King George Palace < ────────
T-Palace@Classical King George Palace

Syntagma Square •

Plaka

• Roman Agora
• Tower of the Winds

Kanellopoulou Museum •

• Ancient Agora

Herodes Atticus Amphitheatre •

Makriagianni

• Filopappou Hill

Koukaki

Kallirrois

Elefth. Venizelou

• Theatre Lykavittos
Greek National Opera

Stadiou *Panepistimiou*

Kolonaki

• Kolonaki Square

Vas. Sophias Avenue

• Greek Folk Art Museum

• Frissiras Museum

• Acropolis
• Theatre Dionysou

• Temple of Olympian Zeus
• Hadrian's Arch

• Lykavittos Hill

Kifissias Avenue

War Museum

Byzantine Museum

Vas. Constantinos Avenue

Pagrati

• Panathenaic Stadium

Mets

Ymittou

Syngrou Avenue   *Amvrosiou*

• Kallitheas Stadium

0 km 0.2 0.4 0.8 km

athens + greater attica

'We do not imitate, but are a model to others', Pericles famously said during the Golden Age of Athens (circa 5th century BC)—a quote that still holds true today, more than two thousand years in the future. What the Athenians have created over the years—in addition to their sizable contributions to drama, democracy, language and philosophy—is, arguably, one of the greatest cities and civilisations in the world.

Home to over five million people, Athens easily ranks as a bustling metropolis based on population alone. When one considers the city's archaeological sites, museums, ritzy beach resorts, eclectic shopping, exciting nightlife and iconic cuisine, it's easy to see how Athens received its reputation.

Athens has certainly endured its fair share of criticism over the years. Like many urban areas around the globe, the city's population exploded during the 20th century. The first demographic shock came with the signing of the Treaty of Lausanne in 1923, when the number of inhabitants skyrocketed with the expulsion of Greeks from Turkey during a compulsory mutual population exchange between the two countries. In all, some 1,500,000 Greeks living in Asia Minor, Anatolia and Eastern Thrace were repatriated. The second demographic shock came after WW II—hundreds of thousands flooded in from the countryside during the subsequent economic boom. These new Athenians brought with them a spate of social problems associated with rapid urban growth—traffic congestion, air pollution and drab housing became the city's hallmarks by the 1970s. The situation escalated to such dire proportions that tourists started skipping the Hellenic capital in favour of the Greek isles or the hinterland.

extreme makeover, athens style

Circumstances did not improve until after 1981, when Greece was admitted into the European Community (later Union) as its tenth member. Membership in the EU meant more money for infrastructure and education, among other areas, but it also pulled the country into the European mainstream. In spite of their misgivings with Greece's new position, Greeks found that they could now travel, work and live abroad more easily, and many brought home with them new ideas and a zest for social change. Slowly but surely, Athens began to sort out its issues. Combined with the individual efforts of a new generation of well-heeled Greeks, the city soon shook off its archaic image and transformed into the fast-paced, cosmopolitan capital it is today.

THIS PAGE (FROM TOP): *Athens revamped its subway system, built a brand new airport and created spectacular sports venues for the 2004 Olympics; similar to sports fans all around the globe, Greeks are known for their ardent support of the home teams.*

PAGE 46: *Perched on Attica's southeastern extreme, the ancient Temple of Poseidon at Cape Sounion basks in the late afternoon light.*

...an icon of western civilisation...

The city's demographics also experienced another dramatic shift, not so much in sheer numbers—the population of the central zone has actually decreased significantly over the last 20 years—but in terms of ethnic mix. The disintegration of Yugoslavia and the liberation of other East European countries from communism sparked an influx of foreigners to Athens searching for work and a better life. Today, it is common to encounter Eastern Europeans and even South Asians working and living in Athens.

Within a decade, Athens shed its outdated image and became a modern, sophisticated model of the 1990s, complete with all of the commercial centres, luxury shopping, nightlife and culture one associates with the world's great capitals. The final push came before the 2004 Summer Olympic Games, when billions of euros were invested by the European Union and the Greek government to develop a new airport and mass transit system, and to revamp the city's roads and parks—necessary infrastructure that has made Athens easy to navigate for visitors and residents alike. The *coup de grâce* was morphing much of central Athens into a massive traffic-free, pedestrian zone.

Although traditional Greek lifestyles have largely merged with that of their European neighbours over the past generation, it's still possible to see elderly men sipping *ouzo* in sidewalk cafés and black-clad widows slipping into Orthodox churches to pray. And as the riots of late 2008 demonstrated, Athenians have certainly not lost their celebrated penchant for anarchy. Nowadays, Athens is really made of three dramatically different parts—the ancient city centred around the Acropolis; a bustling city centre that includes a modern downtown business district and trendy neighbourhoods such as Kolonaki, Plaka and Monastiraki; and a ring of middle-class and posh upscale suburbs such as Kifissia and Ekali and larger cities that now stretch far into the surrounding regions of Attica.

ancient athens

Founded circa 2500 BC, Athens is one of the world's oldest cities. By the 5th century BC, it had surpassed all the other Greek city-states—including its archrival Sparta—to become the leading military, economic and cultural leader of the ancient world. From the beginning, life in Athens focused on and around a distinctive epicentre called the Acropolis. Over several centuries, the flat-topped hill evolved from a fortified citadel into a religious centre dedicated to the goddess Athena. Along with the Statue of Liberty and the Eiffel Tower, the 150-m (490-ft) monument remains one of the greatest accomplishments of western civilisation and a hub of local life.

New excavations of the Acropolis have yielded so many ancient treasures that the existing Acropolis Museum lacked the space to display them all; to this end, the New Acropolis Museum was built. In addition to its artefacts, the new museum has allocated and set aside a specific space for the

THIS PAGE (FROM TOP): *Athens is the fulcrum of the Greek Orthodox faith, personified by its many churches and solemn ceremonies; Evzones troops (presidential guards) on their way to the Changing of the Guard ceremony in Syntagma Square.*
OPPOSITE: *From graffiti murals to posh galleries, Athens has become a hub of modern art.*

Parthenon Marbles, also known as the Elgin Marbles—a collection of classical Greek marble sculptures and figures—in hopes that they will some day be returned to Greece. For now, the collection resides controversially at the British Museum in London. Built at a cost of 130 million euros and designed by Swiss architect Bernard Tschumi, the new museum is located in the flatlands to the south of the plateau, with full-length windows through which superb panoramas of the Acropolis can be viewed.

Later civilisations created their own versions of Athens on the plain north of the Acropolis. The Byzantines—far more interested in developing their new capital of Constantinople—left Athens to go to seed. After Emperor Justinian ordered the closure of the School of Philosophy in 529 AD, the city lost its last great reason for existence. Athens regained a little of its former glory after it was captured by the Ottomans in 1456. The Acropolis became the centre of Ottoman power and the Parthenon served as a mosque for nearly 400 years. It remained in pristine condition until the Ottoman—Venetian war of 1687 destroyed the roof. The slopes and flatlands north of the Acropolis is where Greek commoners lived during both Byzantine and Ottoman times, a bustling residential and commercial area that came to be called the Plaka.

Nowadays, the lovely Plaka, Monastiraki and Psirri neighbourhoods encompass the heart of historical Athens, a must-visit area enroute to the Acropolis. Plaka in particular, is known for its narrow streets and charming red-roofed buildings, although nowadays they are more likely to house restaurants, bars and shops than bona-fide residents. Visitors with little experience of the country may want to be careful, as some establishments here fit the label of 'tourist trap'; regardless, Plaka continues to be the place to experience traditional Greek cuisine and music.

THIS PAGE: *Among the historic structures that cluster around the Acropolis are the Herodes Atticus Amphitheatre (left) and the Parthenon (centre).*

OPPOSITE: *Athens old and new— an Orthodox priest ambles past a fashion billboard in the central business district.*

modern athens

Life in the central business district revolves around Vasilissis Sofias and Kifissias Avenues. Traffic swirls around Omonia Square, while underground lies one of the city's busiest metro stations. Nearby is the University of Athens and Exarchia, a student neighbourhood overflowing with bohemian cafés and clubs, and also home to the National Museum of Archaeology.

Kolonaki district is brimming with stylish boutiques, restaurants and art galleries. The scene retains an air of sophistication; Kolonaki is where local celebrities and socialites congregate, and it is on the Tsakalof and Voukourestiou Streets—fondly known as the 'Rodeo Drive of Athens'—that denizens are much more likely to don designer frocks than frayed jeans. A funicular railway rises from Kolonaki to the summit of Lykavettos Hill, whose elevated vantage point from the Church of St George offers unhindered bird's eye views of the city.

Due to the 2004 Olympics, rundown inner city neighbourhoods that have been given a makeover are still experiencing a renaissance. Psirri has evolved into a district of trendy bars and live music venues. Gazi sports an even hipper vibe thanks to uber-cool clubs and cutting-edge restaurants. Down the road from Gazi is the futuristic Hellenic Foundation for Culture, showcasing Greek history through the ages via virtual reality, hands-on exhibits and film screenings.

the attica coast

The capital's rich hinterland, Attica was once nothing more than a quarry from which Athens drew its marble and precious metals. Such nondescript circumstances is soon to be a thing of the past, and modern Attica is now gaining prominence for its chic beach resorts and posh villas.

The local bourgeoisie have called the fertile region home since the late 1800s and its popularity—and price—continued to increase throughout the 20th century as inner city Athens became overcrowded. The terrain varies widely from posh suburbs and rocky beaches, to idyllic vineyards, pine forests and architectural icons such as the 70,000-seat Olympic Stadium in Maroussi—whose arched roof is designed by famous Spanish architect Calatrava.

The Attica Coast along the eastern shore of the Saronic Gulf is especially chic. With its bevy of private yachts and edgy waterfront cafés, Vouliagmeni is the epitome of a jet-setter hangout. The seaside town is also known for its therapeutic waters and award-winning beaches; the coast has consistently been awarded European Union Blue Flags for environmental excellence. Atticans are also known for their aquatic prowess. Regularly seen sailing, jet skiing and windsurfing in the main bay, many have also passed through the doors of The Nautical Club of Vouliagmeni to become one of the nation's best waterskiers and waterpolo players.

Lagonissi epitomises new-wave hip and draws a younger, more vibrant crowd, especially during the sultry summer months when the party scene often continues after dawn. Lagonissi's relaxed island ambience is the main lure for many looking to escape Athens' urban nature while the municipality's proximity to the capital sees many celebrities building their luxury villas here. Despite its modern image, the area also has its ancient attractions. Long ago, pilgrims of a much different sort flocked to the Temple of Poseidon on Cape Sounion. One of the most photographed landmarks in Greece, the temple boasts 15 Doric columns and glittering views of the Aegean.

northern attica

The Battle of Marathon between Athenians and the Persian Army played out on the plains of northern Attica in 490 BC. The bloody encounter changed not only the history of Greece but also all of western civilisation, preserving Athenian culture and democracy. Several monuments mark the battlefield today, including the burial mound of Athenians killed in the conflict. The battle also became renowned for the 40 km (25 miles) covered by Athenian soldier Fidipidis in order to bring home news of victory. Fidipidis' tenacity and subsequent death (he died from exhaustion) emphasised the soldier's strength of character, and the Olympic Games' most gruelling event—the marathon—derives its name from this occasion.

The vast, man-made Lake Marathónas—near the posh suburb of Ekali—is where the Athenian wealthy make their home. There are several interesting sights in the area, including the Yiannis Spyropoulos Museum of Art and the Spathário Museum of Shadow Theatre. The former showcases the artwork of one of the nation's foremost 20th-century artists, while the latter is dedicated to traditional Greek shadow puppetry.

THIS PAGE: The coast of Attica is known for its seaside luxuries and relaxed pace of life.

OPPOSITE: The funicular railway that travels up to the crest of Lykavettos Hill reveals startling views of the capital at night.

...modern Attica is now gaining prominence for its chic beach resorts and posh villas.

athens life gallery

Does Art imitate Life, or is it the other way around? Can works of art change the way we perceive our environments? The bluegr Mamidakis hotel group has attempted to answer these questions with the creation of the Athens Life Gallery hotel, a living space fused with the aesthetic offerings of the finest Greek and international artists.

Located in Athens, ensconced within the stylish suburb of Ekali, the Athens Life Gallery is renowned for being as much an art gallery as a luxury hotel. Designed to enhance the appreciation of its contents, the hotel inhabits a minimalist frame with tasteful, subdued décor—Zen gardens, soothing pools and the subtle use of candles and ethnic designs. Locked away in its leafy suburban nest, the property's dedication to privacy makes it seem more like a modern country retreat than a boutique hotel in the city.

The relative solitude and restrained décor creates a space perfect for contemplating the hotel's museum-quality exhibition of artwork and sculptures. Displayed year-round and refreshed on a regular basis, it features some of the most exciting names in modern Greek art. Nikos Alexiou, Nikos Kessanlis, George Lappas, Takis and George Giparakis are just some artists who have applied their unique visions and talents.

Every facet of the Athens Life Gallery hotel's appearance and function has been crafted to create a greater whole. Throughout its 24 Deluxe Rooms, three Art Studio rooms, and two Junior Suites, the hotel's living spaces exude a cool sense of style. Followers of modern furniture will recognise some of the chic designer pieces seen throughout the building. Every room has a subtle lighting scheme and a small collection of remarkable artworks and *objets d'art*. Marvel at the luxe amenities, comfortable beds, minibars, desks, and other features by such names as Bang & Olufsen, Phillips, Electrolux and Cocomat.

At the Wine Gallery, over 200 varieties of wine are on offer, representing all the world's major producing regions. A special menu of food prepared from seasonal ingredients is designed to elicit the best possible responses when paired with the cellar's offerings.

Surrounding the main structure are a series of landscaped walking gardens, broken by the presence of two large swimming pools. The property also features Ananea Spa, its name derived from the Greek word for renewal. Built from Serena marble, the spa features a range of facilities, including a deeply inspiring Meditation Room. All treatments use an exclusive range of 100-percent organic products, and are performed in beautiful suites and surroundings to help calm the spirit. From Thai massage to reiki healing hot stones, a visit to the Ananea Spa is the perfect way to prepare one's senses before a tour of the unforgettable galleries.

If ever it was said that art cannot change the way we see life, then the Athens Life Gallery hotel is an instinctive response painted in bold strokes.

rooms
24 rooms • 3 Art Studios • 2 Junior Suites

food
Wine Gallery: dishes paired with wine

drink
Wine Gallery: over 200 varieties of wine • Pisco Sour Bar

features
Ananea Spa • art and sculpture collections • 2 pools • landscaped gardens • gym

nearby
Kifissia • Maroussi • shops • nightlife

contact
103 Thisseos Avenue, Ekali, 14578 Athens • telephone: +30.210.626 0400 • facsimile: +30.210.622 9353 • email: info-lifegallery@bluegr.com • website: www.bluegr.com

classical 2, fashion house hotel

In the heart of Athens, occupying a prime location in the trendy downtown district, lies the Classical 2, Fashion House Hotel. Its excellent situation places it within convenient walking distance of anything of interest for regular visitors and new tourists alike.

With its colourful wrap-around stained-glass balconies, the nine-storey structure immediately catches the eye—more than just a building, the hotel is a huge modern work of art that dazzles the downtown cityscape.

Completely refurbished in 2008, the hotel boasts 110 guestrooms and suites. Averaging 26–30 sq m (280–323 sq ft) in size, rooms were individually styled by contemporary Greek designers, photographers and artists—including such names as Michalis Pantos, Vaso Konsola, Elena Zournatzi, Vassilis Zoulias

and Victoria Kyriakides—who were essentially given carte blanche to craft quarters that were both comfortable and creative.

One never quite knows what to expect, but that's part of the allure at the Classical 2, Fashion House Hotel. The décor includes vivid colours mixed with period furniture, vintage photographs, graffiti, quirky wallpapers, *objets d'art* and some items that are plainly bizarre. An eclectic mix, to be sure, but rather than looking out of place, all of them come together to create a lively atmosphere.

Every room offers stunning views of the city and Likavitos Hill. Amenities include LCD televisions with satellite channels, iPod docking stations, mobile phones and complimentary wireless Internet access. Smoking and non-smoking rooms are both

THIS PAGE (FROM LEFT): Psychedelic stained-glass balconies make Classical 2, Fashion House Hotel immediately recognisable; rooms can be considered works of art in their own right.

OPPOSITE (FROM LEFT): The Fashion Airways Café is designed to mirror a private Lear Jet; the hotel's creative design extends even to the carpets.

available. Suites flaunt the same bohemian design sense, with open-plan layouts that feature separate sitting areas and queen beds strategically placed near the windows, so one can enjoy the stunning urban views.

Rooms come equipped with Tina's *Black Book*, a guide-cum-directory to Athens, with addresses and phone numbers for everything from malls, bookshops and theatres to more eccentric establishments like cranial masseurs, costume rental shops and blood-test centres. Entries also include commentary and personal anecdotes, helpful for first-time visitors.

The hotel's whimsical character continues downstairs. 'Fly away' in a private jet at the Fashion Airways Café—complete with bulkheads, portholes and a giant route map to the world's leading fashion destinations. Here, passengers can enjoy a variety of pastries, snacks, cocktails, coffees and teas.

One floor up is the FooDBall Restaurant, a sports-themed bar and restaurant. The décor features a bright green 'soccer field' floor and life-sized sports photographs.

For guests with a more serious mission in mind, the Classical 2, Fashion House Hotel also boasts a 24-hour business centre with secretarial and translation services, as well as conference and banquet facilities decked out with the latest audiovisual gadgets.

Even on foot, the hotel is just a few minutes from the trendy Kolonaki district and Plaka neighbourhood. For a taste of history, head to the Acropolis and its surrounding antiquities, which include temples, theatres, cemeteries and an ancient market place. The metro station is almost at the hotel's doorstep, while Athens International Airport is only 35 km (15 miles) away: trivial by car, and a mere 45-minute ride by metro.

rooms
110 rooms and suites

food
FooDBall Restaurant: international • Fashion Airways Café: snacks

drink
FooDBall Restaurant • Fashion Airways Café

features
wireless Internet access • laptop and printer rentals • conference and banquet facilities • 24-hour business centre • translation and secretarial services • guru, fortune teller and nanny services by request • stylist • personal buyer • direct metro access • smoking and non-smoking rooms

nearby
Acropolis • Plaka • metro station • museums • restaurants • shopping • theatres • nightlife

contact
2 Pireos Street, 10552 Athens • telephone: +30.210.523 5230 • facsimile: +30.210.523 4955 • email: 2fhh@classicalhotels.com • website: www.classicalhotels.com

classical babygrand hotel

away that this is a hotel that doesn't take itself too seriously, and the whimsical vibe continues through to the guestrooms.

Fifty-four of the 76 rooms are graffiti themed; one room has Spiderman peeking out from behind the curtains, while the Smurftown-themed room features Smurfs running amok. As each room is an individual piece of art decorated by a different Greek artist, no two are the same. Not all feature cartoon characters; other themes include enormous olives that seem to bounce off the walls, leaping dolphins, and Oriental landscapes complete with waterfalls and cloud-enshrouded peaks.

For those with more sedate tastes, 20 Classical rooms feature traditional décor, from Art Deco to European modern. Junior suites offer panoramic city views overlooking Kotzia Square; they also have a separate, open-plan sitting area. Business suites are available for

Rooms decorated with cartoon characters and graffiti; front desks that could seemingly double as a getaway car; birds chirping in the corridors. Is this a place to stay or some real-life version of a Salvador Dali painting? Actually it's a little of both—the Classical BabyGrand Hotel in downtown Athens is as surreal as it gets here in the Greek capital.

Dubbed one of the 'best new places to stay in the world' by *Condé Nast Traveller*, the hotel is situated midway between Omonia Square and the Monastiraki district—the crossroads of Athens' business and leisure centres. Upon stepping inside, one is greeted by Mini Cooper desks and psychedelic 1960s-style wallpaper. It becomes obvious right

THIS PAGE (FROM LEFT): Walking into the hotel is almost like entering a surrealist painting; Moet & Chandon Bar features eccentric objets d'art.

OPPOSITE (FROM LEFT): No two rooms in the hotel are the same; with soft lighting, quiet music, and a range of treatments, the spa soothes and relaxes.

those coming to Athens for professional reasons; they offer a sizable work room with a desk, bookshelf and all the high-tech accessories one needs to stay connected.

Regardless of the room type, they all come with customised touches such as iPods with hip playlists and individual pieces of art. All rooms have marble bathrooms; other amenities include wireless Internet, in-room safes, and satellite TV.

The fun continues at the Moet & Chandon Bar with its oversized leather sofas, splashes of vivid colour and eccentric *objets d'art*—ostrich tables, mirrored bead curtains, and Ming vases. Those enjoying a romantic night out will enjoy sipping champagne from intertwined champagne flutes, while soft music and tasty finger foods set the mood for hotel guests and trendy Athenians.

For a change of pace, the BabyGrand restaurant unfolds as a jungle of white plastic flowers and vines. Buffet breakfasts are exceptional and the à la carte cuisine is a new take on the traditional Greek taverna with gourmet kebabs, burgers, steaks and salads.

Classical Spa CARITA offers relief from jet lag, with a refreshing marble hammam and treatments ranging from aromatherapy and reflexology to caviar body elixirs and spirulina seaweed facials. If one feels guilty after indulging at the restaurant or bar, there is also an exercise area and an indoor pool.

rooms
65 rooms · 11 suites

food
BabyGrand Restaurant: Greek taverna

drink
Moet & Chandon Bar

features
Classical Spa CARITA: indoor pool, beauty salon, gym, hammam · complimentary wireless Internet access · business centre · meeting and function facilities · secretarial and translation services · audiovisual equipment · direct metro access · smoking and non-smoking rooms

nearby
Kotzia Square · Monastiraki district · Omonia Square · shopping malls · restaurants · cafés

contact
65 Athinas & Lycourgou Street, 10551 Athens · telephone: +30.210.325 0900 · facsimile: +30.210.325 0920 · email: bg@classicalhotels.com · website: www.classicalhotels.com

classical king george palace

One of Athens' landmark hotels, the Classical King George Palace has played host to the world's elite since its grand opening in 1936. Totally refurbished for the 2004 Summer Games, the lavish property boasts 102 rooms but feels more like an intimate boutique hotel.

Ranked among the '100 Top European Hotels' by *Condé Nast Traveler* magazine, the building was originally a grand, private mansion. It is situated close to the former royal palace (now the Greek Parliament) on Syntagma Square, also known as Constitution Square. The hotel skilfully juxtaposes old with new, as in the case of the T-Palace lounge, a wholly modern rendezvous for food, cocktails and music.

Upstairs at Classical King George Palace, unique guestrooms and suites feature period furniture, antiques and plush upholstery. Spacious bathrooms in grey marble flaunt sunken tubs and glass-encased showers.

Amenities include down comforters, a pillow menu and 24-hour room service. High-tech offerings run from CD players and plasma TVs to wireless high-speed Internet access, multi-line telephones, laptop and printer loans, and refrigerators with snacks from Agreco, the upmarket Athenian grocer.

Many rooms have balconies overlooking the hotel's inner courtyard or Syntagma Square. Suites have it even better—the two-bedroom King George Suite offers stunning

THIS PAGE (FROM LEFT): Guests of the Royal Penthouse Suite can enjoy views of the Acropolis; rooms are appointed with opulent period furniture.

OPPOSITE (FROM LEFT): Enjoy Greco-French cuisine at Tudor Hall; artist Konstantinos Kakanias has lent his talents to many of the artworks at the hotel.

rooms
78 rooms • 23 suites • 1 Royal Penthouse Suite

food
Tudor Hall: Greco-French •
T-Palace: international and sushi

drink
T-Palace: lounge

features
Charisma Jewelry Store • health club • fitness centre • spa • beauty salon • indoor pool • Internet access • grand ballroom • conference and meeting rooms • audiovisual equipment • 24-hour business corner with two working stations • secretarial and translation services • direct metro access • smoking and non-smoking rooms

nearby
Kolonaki • Syntagma Square • Plaka district • Acropolis • sporting facilities

contact
3 Vasiliou Georgiou 1st Street
Syntagma Square, 10564 Athens •
telephone: +30.210.322 2210 •
facsimile: +30.210.325 0504 •
email: kgpalace@classicalhotels.com •
website: www.classicalhotels.com

views of the Acropolis, the Greek Parliament and the city of Athens; inside, it is furnished with rare antiques and original artwork.

The Royal Penthouse Suite on the 9th floor redefines luxury with original artwork by Konstantinos Kakanias, a private elevator and separate entrances for guests and staff. The suite has a private terrace with panoramic city views, a jacuzzi and even a private pool. Penthouse guests are also privy to a butler and limousine service. Famous guests of the suite have included Aristotle Onassis, Marilyn Monroe and Frank Sinatra.

The hotel's famed Tudor Hall restaurant boasts a Greco-French menu. Guests can choose to sit inside among tasteful opulence or on the al fresco terrace to fully enjoy the balmy Greek evening. While dining here, one shouldn't be surprised to see politicians, diplomats or international celebrities sitting at adjacent tables.

Open to guests only, the health club features a gym, indoor pool, whirlpool, steam bath, sauna and two treatment rooms. The concierge desk can also arrange off-site recreation including tennis, squash, jogging, golf, horseback riding and trips to the beach.

The Classical King George Palace is within easy walking distance of the Acropolis and the Acropolis Museum, half a dozen other museums, as well as the lively Plaka district, while across the street is a metro station with a direct link to the airport, making this a premium choice for discerning tourists.

grand resort lagonissi

Offering 291 rooms and suites spread over a vast 29 hectares (72 acres) of lush greenery, and no less than 12 crescent-shaped private beaches surrounded by the shimmering Aegean Sea, luxury is unrivalled at the Grand Resort Lagonissi. With a private helipad and docking jetty, one can arrive in style by sailing right up to the doorstep of this dream resort.

A 40-minute limousine drive away from the centre of Athens, Grand Resort Lagonissi redefines luxury travel and living for even the most well-heeled traveller. The resort is a member of the prestigious 'Leading Hotels of the World' group, and provides no less than five levels of accommodation, ranging from luxurious to extravagant.

Couples longing for a romantic stay can enjoy their intimate moments in the Dream Suite. The aptly named suite has an unusual feature: a remote-controlled retractable ceiling above the king-sized bed. When activated, the seemingly solid roof unveils a glass skylight, allowing one to gaze on a vista of azure skies or a blanket of stars.

Families can enjoy a rolling good time in the spacious Residence Villa. The villa comes with a fully equipped kitchen and a sprawling private garden which allows children to play freely without fear of disturbing other guests. For the ultra-rich guest who expects nothing less than the ultimate experience, there is the Royal Suite. Fit for kings, the suite is adorned with designer furniture and state-of-the-art technology. It also comes with a fully equipped business centre with modern facilities such as a laptop and videophone, so jet-setting businessmen can stay in touch with their colleagues. Guests of the suite also enjoy the services of a personal butler, a private chef, pianist and personal trainer upon request.

Dining at the Grand Resort Lagonissi is equally impressive. With a selection of 12 award-winning restaurants serving an array of international cuisine, diners are spoilt for choice. Head to Ouzeri for authentic Greek specialities, while Captain's House serves fine

rooms
92 rooms • 199 bungalows, suites and villas

food
Ouzeri: Greek • Captain's House: Italian • Kohylia Restaurant & Sushi Bar: Polynesian • Poseidon Restaurant: Greek • Veghera Club Restaurant: international • Galazia Akti: contemporary Greek • Mediterraneo: light meals • Aphrodite: international

drink
Veghera • Captain's Deck • The Veranda Bar • Grand Pier • La Piscine

features
ThalaSpa Chenot • outdoor pool • 12 private beaches • gym • fitness centre • watersports • tennis courts • parasailing • private jet and helicopter services • meeting facilities

nearby
Temple of Poseidon • beaches • golf courses

contact
40th Km Athens-Sounion Avenue 19010 Lagonissi, Athens • telephone: +30.22.9107 6000 • facsimile: +30.22.9102 4534 • email: reservations@grandresort.gr • website: www.grandresort.gr

Italian food with unparalleled views of the sea. For more adventurous palates, Kohylia offers unique Polynesian and sushi delicacies. Those who just can't decide should try the international buffets at Aphrodite. In-room dining can also be arranged for guests who want to dine in the privacy of their own suite.

Visitors can pamper themselves at the ThalaSpa Chenot. The spa helps guests create a bespoke treatment menu from a full range of therapies to best suit their needs, and their Bio-light menu offers healthy and innovative dishes. Those who prefer to stay active may choose to sweat it out at the fitness centre or rough it out on the seas with sailing, scuba diving or windsurfing. With 12 private beaches along the peninsula, sunbathers can choose a new venue from which to enjoy the warm sun every day. Private transportation to sites of interest can also be arranged. Guests can visit the nearby Temple of Poseidon, whose magnificent columns soar high above the sea. Stay until evening to catch the gorgeous sunset—a phenomenon forever immortalised in Lord Byron's poems. Yachts can also be hired for a private cruise to the surrounding islands.

For a perfect sun-drenched holiday at a venue which spares no effort to ensure the enjoyment of its guests, look no further than the Grand Resort Lagonissi.

grecotel cape sounio

Standing at the southern tip of the Greek mainland, across an azure bay from the Temple of Poseidon, lies the Grecotel Cape Sounio. Situated on the edge of Cape Sounio National Park, the resort's terracotta villas blend effortlessly into a landscape of olive groves, rocky shoreline and pine forest.

The cape's ecological resources allow for a natural classroom and laboratory experience where guests can learn appreciation for nature as well as attain an understanding of how sustainability can be continued back home. To this end, the resort has partnered with oceanographer Jean-Michel Cousteau to offer an 'Ambassadors of the Environment' program to give younger guests a better understanding of their role in the planet's ecosystem through activities like kayaking, rock climbing and snorkelling.

The resort's open-plan bungalows offer sea, temple or parkland views through floor-to-ceiling glass doors. Rooms are decorated in earth tones, with a master bedroom as well as sofa bed in the living area. The one- and two-bedroom villas are individually decorated with handcrafted furniture and designer fabrics. They also feature private terraces and gardens—many with private pools.

Located near the peak of Royal Hill, the two-bedroom Pine Hill Villa is set in a private pine forest with landscaped grounds. Superb views of the temple and cape can be enjoyed

THIS PAGE (FROM LEFT): At Yali, couples can savour romantic candlelit meals over the waterfront; water features enhance the view from the lobby terrace.

OPPOSITE (FROM LEFT): The wealth of marine life around the resort makes it ideal for nature lovers; villas feature handcrafted furniture and lush fabrics.

rooms
149 bungalows, villas, residences and estate

food
Cape Sounio Restaurant: international •
So Oriental: Asian fusion • Cavo Kolones: Cretan
and organic • Yali: seafood and Mediterranean •
Aegean Grill: light meals

drink
Lounge bar and terraces

features
Elixir Spa 007 • outdoor saltwater pool •
glass-walled indoor pools• kids' program •
private yacht • meeting and function rooms

nearby
Temple of Poseidon •
Cape Sounio National Park

contact
67 Km Athens–Sounio Road
19500 Sounio, Attica •
telephone: +30.22.9206 9700 •
facsimile: +30.22.9206 9770 •
email: reserv_so@grecotel.gr •
website: www.capesounio.com

from the outdoor lounge. The opulent interior boasts a walk-in closet, two marble baths and a hospitality room for coffee and tea service.

But the resort's crowning glory is the Cape Sounio Estate, which comprises six separate but closely linked villas that can accommodate as many as eight guests. The estate boasts three pools, private gardens and forest land, parking for four cars, personal housekeeping and gardening services, priority tennis court access and club car transfer within the resort grounds.

The Cape Sounio Restaurant offers the best in Greek and international cuisine along with spectacular views. Asian fusion dishes are served up at the elegant So Oriental. Cavo Colones showcases the culinary traditions of Crete, dishes prepared with fresh products direct from Grecotel's own organic farm. Fresh seafood is the forté at the laid-back Yali Waterfront Cabanas Restaurant.

The octagon-shaped Elixir Spa 007 was inspired by the James Bond blockbuster, Dr No, and features glass exterior walls to enhance the sensation of being outdoors. The atmosphere inside exudes total calm with scented candles, recessed lighting and chakra-balancing music. Ayurverda treatments are performed by Indian experts, but the spa menu also includes aromatherapy, reflexology and energising lymph draining massages. Some of the exotic treatment options include caviar, chocolate and crystals as well as 'Love Potions' for couples.

hilton athens

A landmark building in the city of Athens since its construction in 1963, the Hilton Athens was one of the first high-rise structures to be erected in the prestigious downtown area. From its lofty perch on Vassilissis Sofias Avenue, the 13-storey hotel has clear views across the city's spectacular boulevards all the way to the Acropolis. No other establishment can boast of the Hilton's 179 Acropolis-facing rooms, or its experience in providing flawless vacations and business trips.

Its location not only affords the Hilton Athens remarkable views—other guestrooms overlook Lycabettus Hill and the Hymettus mountain range—but also convenient access to the city's rich sights and museums. After

arriving at Athens International Airport, most guests will be able to check in and hit the town within an hour. The popular shopping district of Kolonaki can be reached on foot, and those with an interest in archaeological sites can make a stop at the Acropolis, just a 10-minute cab ride from the front steps.

In all, there are 508 guestrooms and suites under the Hilton's roof. Seventy-four of them are new additions from a recent renovation that added a new northern wing and also overhauled the hotel's interiors. Comfort and classic design meet the eye at every turn.

The standard Hilton Guest Room is the result of careful consideration and planning by the hotel giant, meeting the needs of

THIS PAGE (FROM LEFT): The spacious living room of the Presidential Suite is equally suited for an informal meeting or a party; enjoy a drink on Galaxy Bar's terrace on a summer evening.

OPPOSITE (FROM LEFT): The Galaxy Bar serves chic cocktails and is a great place to meet people; relax with a dip in one of the Hilton Athens' swimming pools.

modern travellers without sacrificing luxury, aesthetic refinement or space. Each room comes complete with a seating area, balcony and working desk. Amenities include satellite TV channels on LCD screens, high-speed Internet access, two direct-dial telephones, and marble bathrooms with soaking tubs and separate walk-in showers. For access to a lounge where complimentary breakfasts and refreshments are served daily, they are also available as Hilton Executive Rooms.

Impressive as the standard rooms may be, each of the Hilton Athens' 34 suites expand horizons when it comes to luxurious extras. The King Acropolis Suite has two bedrooms, a living room that doubles as a DVD theatre, a separate dining room and a panoramic view of the Acropolis from its balcony. The apartment-sized King Presidential Suite tops them all with its 218 sq m (2,347 sq ft) of opulence that boasts a bar, dining table, jacuzzi, sauna and fully equipped kitchen.

For relaxation, the hotel offers the largest outdoor pool in the city, itself just one of three pools available. The fitness centre contains one other, along with a sauna, massage, and steam room facilities. It's no wonder local and international celebrities return time after time to the Hilton Athens. Add six restaurants and bars to the mix, such as the exemplary Greek establishment, Milos, and one is left with a recipe for Athens served up in style.

rooms
508 rooms including 34 suites

food
Milos: traditional Greek • Oasis Bar & Grill: Mediterranean • Byzantine: modern Mediterranean • Aethrion Lounge: Japanese • Galaxy Roof Restaurant: international

drink
Galaxy Bar • Aethrion Lounge

features
Executive Lounge • 24-hour room service • fitness centre • spa • 3 pools • Internet access • 22 meeting rooms

nearby
Athens Acropolis • Temple of Olympian Zeus • museums • shops • tennis and squash • cinemas

contact
46 Vassilissis Sofias Avenue, 11528 Athens • telephone: +30.210.728 1000 • facsimile: +30.210.728 1111 • email: pr.athens@hilton.com • website: www.hiltonathens.gr

island club + restaurant

Nothing can bring people together better than good food, wine and atmosphere, and diners can revel in all three at the classy Island Club & Restaurant in Athens.

Amid historical monuments and works of art in the vibrant capital of Greece, this club-restaurant blends in with effortless style. Walls are painted white, reminiscent of traditional Cycladic architecture, and feature modern Mediterranean art. With high ceilings and expansive premises, Island is the perfect place to end the day, either with a fine meal or by listening to music at the club.

When it first opened in 1994, Island offered Mediterranean cuisine, a menu that expanded and took a new creative turn as innovative Greek chefs came to the kitchen. Fans of Asian cuisine can also enjoy fresh sushi, prepared by Japanese chefs. After a meal, wind down with drinks at the Tapas Lounge, located under a covered patio that almost feels like one is stepping into Spain. The club even has its own a wine cellar that houses over 150 different types of local and international wine, while a trained sommelier is on hand to help one choose the perfect vintage.

Apart from the alluring ambience and succulent food, Island Club & Restaurant is an ideal place for holding private receptions, with its five separate areas—the Residence, Gallery, Prive, C-Lounge and the Private House.

Set in a lush garden, surrounded by softly lit olive trees and tamarisks, the Residence has a romantic air. It can seat up to 1,000 diners,

and with tables set right up to the water's edge, one can expect breathtaking views under starry skies.

For a quieter dinner, head to the Gallery, which can accommodate 400 guests on different terraces. With views of a church sitting on the rocks by the sea nearby, Gallery enjoys a serene and tranquil atmosphere.

The Prive section is decked out in modern Mediterranean features in a large verandah with magnificent views of the sea. It seats up to 100, making it an ideal choice to hold corporate dinners or events.

If one is hosting an even more exclusive gathering, choose the intimate C-Lounge. Juxtaposing high-end minimalist furniture from such names as Philippe Starck with rare antique finds from far-flung countries such as Sri Lanka, it makes an intriguing space to host engaging discussions and conversations.

Last but not least, for that professional conference meeting, the Private House is the place to be. Equipped with state-of-the-art audiovisual facilities, this function room allows business to be conducted smoothly, and in style. There is also a lush garden with a Zen pool for that rejuvenating tea break.

To top it all off, each section has a private entrance and open kitchen, so diners can watch talented chefs at work.

With its gorgeous décor, stunning views, divine food and well-appointed dining areas, Island Club & Restaurant is an obvious choice for both locals and visitors new to Athens.

...gorgeous décor, stunning views, divine food and well-appointed dining areas...

capacity
Residence: 1,000 • Gallery: 400 • Prive: 100 •
Private House: 400 • C-Lounge: 140

food
modern Mediterranean • Japanese •
world cuisine

drink
Cocktail Bar • Tapas Lounge • wine cellar

features
Prive: private dining •
Private House: conference room •
Residence, Gallery and C-Lounge: receptions

nearby
shops • restaurants • sea

contact
27th km of Athens–Sounio Avenue •
telephone: +30.210.965 3563 / +30.210.965 3564 •
facsimile: +30.210.892 5053 •
website: www.islandclubrestaurant.gr •

Island Art & Taste (banquets and conferences)
telephone: +30.210.892 5000 •
facsimile: +30.210.892 5050 •
email: sales@panasgroup.gr
website: www.islandartandtaste.gr
          www.panasgroup.gr

t-palace @ classical king george palace

THIS PAGE: *T-Palace features quirky décor such as lip-shaped sofas.*

OPPOSITE (FROM LEFT): *Dutch design firm Moooi created most of the lounge's offbeat furniture; illumination is provided by eye-catching gun-shaped lamps.*

'Are you chic enough?' asks the cheeky lettering on the wall of the T-Palace—actually a piece of installation art by Konstantinos Kakanias. Anyone visiting this swank lounge bar for the first time certainly has to ask themselves that question.

Ensconced on the ground floor of the Classical King George Palace, the lounge has become a hip spot for casual drinks, after-midnight trysts and just about anything else. It's hard to say what catches the eye first— the horse lamps, 'hot lips' sofa or the chrome stools shaped like faces. All of them would be unusual on their own, but they're absolutely mind blowing when thrown together.

It would take an eccentric mind to give shape to such a place. That would be the renowned Greek interior designer and theatre director Antonis Kalogridis, whose stage resumé includes everything from Shakespeare to A Streetcar Named Desire. He started with a stark white canvas and began adding colour as he saw fit; the end result is a cosmopolitan mélange of textures, hues and images.

Kalogridis had help, of course. The horse lamps come from Dutch design firm Moooi, as do the black leather armchairs by Maarten Baas and the Ron Gilad chandelier over the circular Space Bar. Greek artists Konstantinos Kakanias and Dimitris Antonitsis rendered much of the artwork on the walls. New York also leaves its mark, with interior design maestro Philippe Starck and skin artist Scott Campbell, who penned 'I was very good at doing what I was told' on the walls.

The bartenders here have a well-earned reputation for mixing some of Athens' best cocktails. Food is another draw, too, with the selection of Greek dishes and exotic sushi from the Classical King George Palace's kitchen.

The music may be inobtrusive in the afternoon, but it slowly and surely becomes part of the bar's vibe as the clock ticks past midnight. There are also regular DJ shows—the range of different music styles are sure to get one's toes tapping.

T-Palace is also a great place to sit and relax, especially in the afternoon. Kalogridis originally envisioned his creation as a library of sorts, and the lounge makes a tempting—if slightly quirky—spot to enjoy a book while sipping a cappuccino or cool cocktail.

food
Greek and sushi • bar snacks

drink
cocktails from master mixologists

features
regular DJ shows

nearby
Constitution Square • Plaka district • Acropolis • Kolonaki

contact
3 Vassiliou Georgiou 1st Street Syntagma Square, 10564 Athens • telephone: +30.210.322 2210 • facsimile: +30.210.325 0504 • website: www.classicalhotels.com

zoumboulakis galleries

Nations all have their artists and their patrons, and few have done more to promote Greek art over the past century than Zoumboulakis. This art business has expanded from its original location to four spaces around Athens, each with their own speciality.

Zoumboulakis has always been a family-run affair. In 1912, Theodore Zoumboulakis opened one of the most well-known antiques shops in Athens. In the 1960s, his son Tassos Zoumboulakis worked with wife Peggy to open Zoumboulakis Galleries Contemporary Art in collaboration with such international galleries as Alexandre Iolas Gallery and Denise René Gallery. The management and artistic direction of the gallery was later passed to their daughter Daphne, who trained as an art restorer in Britain. Their son, also named Theodore, is a renowned architect who was educated at the University of California. He now maintains his own architectural office in Athens. Theodore has lent his talents to designing several of the gallery spaces.

Contemporary art is the forte of the Zoumboulakis gallery on 20 Kolonaki Square, with works by kinetic sculptor Takis, who inaugurated the space in 1974, and iconic pieces by visual artist Moralis. The gallery also features work from the younger generation of artists, including pieces by Danae Stratou. One of the gallery's most popular annual shows is 'Small Paintings'. The exhibition features small-scale paintings, photography and sculptures by emerging artists as well as artists who have collaborated with the gallery over the years. The show takes place over the Christmas season. Recent solo exhibitions have included 'The End' by Nikos Alexiou, which was shown at the Venice Biennale in 2007; the installation 'The Walking Blind' by Evanthia Tsantila; and 'Electric Home' by Harris Kondosphyris, who represented Greece in the 26th Biennale of Sao Paulo in 2004.

The gallery situated at 7 Kriezotou Street showcases a wide range of limited-edition prints and *objets d'art*, including a selection of modern silk screens by Moralis and prints by Greek painters Christos Bokoros and Giannis Adamakis. This particular Zoumboulakis gallery also exhibits quirky art objects by

galleries
3 galleries • 1 multi-exhibition space

features
contemporary paintings • photographs • sculptures • art shows • art happenings

contact
20 Kolonaki Square, 10673 Athens • telephone: +30.210.360 8278 • facsimile: +30.210.363 1364 • email: galleries@zoumboulakis.gr •

7 Kriezotou Street, 10671 Athens • telephone: +30.210.363 1951 • facsimile: +30.210.362 9980 • email: kriezotou7@zoumboulakis.gr •

6 Kriezotou Street, 10671 Athens • telephone: +30.210.364 0264 • facsimile: +30.210.364 3496 • email: kriezotou6@zoumboulakis.gr •

37 Agathodemonos and 1 Orestrou Street (off 199 Piraeus Street), Athens • telephone: +30.210.341 4214 • website: www.zoumboulakis.gr
www.zone-d.gr

artists such as Diamantis Aidinis, as well as objects by well-known foreign artists like Picasso and Malevich.

Across the street, at 6 Kriezotou Street, offerings at the latest Zoumboulakis gallery comprise an eclectic mix of art, design and antiques. At any given time, the collection can range from 18th-century French furniture and magnetic sculptures to antique toys and rare Rauschenberg pop art lithographs. The space itself could be called a work of art—a striking contrast of dark iron and white, it was conceptualised by Theodore Zoumboulakis.

Located just off Piraeus Street, the Zoumboulakis Art Loft was unveiled in 1995. Originally an old industrial space, the 600-sq-m (6,458-sq-ft) large structure was reshaped by Theodore into a multi-functional space for art and antique shows, theatrical and musical events, and general art-related happenings. It also functions as a workshop to restore and maintain antiques and art.

In addition to its locations around Athens, Zoumboulakis has started an exciting new venture. Launched in 2007, Zone D is a new project curated by Daphne Zoumboulakis. Zone D aims to showcase current trends in the field of international contemporary art in a dynamic context. It evolves with every project, as Zone D utilises different exhibition spaces, and remains flexible according to the needs of each specific exhibition and event.

peloponnese

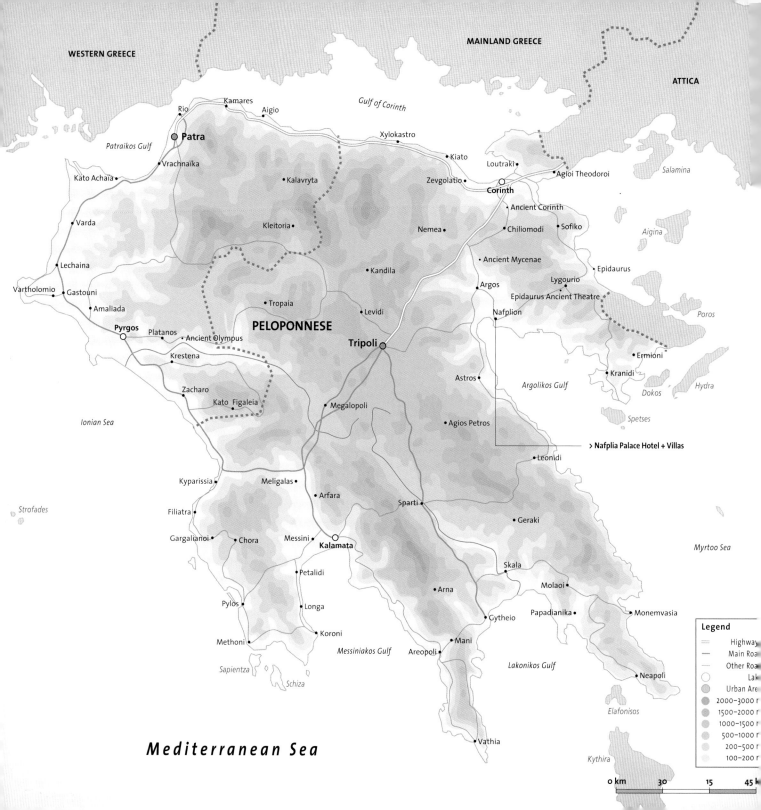

WESTERN GREECE

MAINLAND GREECE

ATTICA

Gulf of Corinth

Kamares
Rio
Aigio
Xylokastro
Patra
Kiato
Vrachnaïka
Loutraki
Agioi Theodoroi
Patraikos Gulf
Zevgolatio
Corinth
Kato Achaïa
Kalavryta
Ancient Corinth
Salamina
Varda
Kleitoria
Nemea
Chiliomodi
Sofiko
Aigina
Ancient Mycenae
Epidaurus
Lechaina
Kandila
Lygourio
Vartholomio
Gastouni
PELOPONNESE
Argos
Epidaurus Ancient Theatre
Poros
Amaliada
Tropaia
Levidi
Nafplion
Pyrgos
Platanos
Tripoli
Ermioni
Ancient Olympus
Kranidi
Krestena
Astros
Argolikos Gulf
Dokos
Hydra
Zacharo
Spetses
Kato Figaleia
Megalopoli
Agios Petros
Ionian Sea
> Nafplia Palace Hotel + Villas
Leonidi
Kyparissia
Meligalas
Strofades
Arfara
Sparti
Filiatra
Myrtoo Sea
Gargalianoi
Chora
Messini
Geraki
Kalamata
Skala
Petalidi
Molaoi
Pylos
Longa
Arna
Monemvasia
Methoni
Koroni
Papadianika
Gytheio
Mani
Messiniakos Gulf
Areopoli
Lakonikos Gulf
Neapoli
Sapientza
Schiza
Elafonisos

Mediterranean Sea

Vathia
Kythira

Legend
Highway
Main Road
Other Road
Lake
Urban Area
2000-3000 m
1500-2000 m
1000-1500 m
500-1000 m
200-500 m
100-200 m

0 km   30   15   45

peloponnese

Fans of obscure military history recognise the Peloponnese as the centrepiece of the eponymous war that played out in the early 5th century BC between Athens and Sparta. But the rugged peninsula, which divides the Aegean and Ionian seas, is known for much more. This was the birthplace of the Olympic games and the birthplace of the Greek Revolution, the war of independence waged against the Ottomans in the 1820s.

Although long renowned for its architectural treasures and viniculture, the Peloponnese has come into its own in recent years as a beach destination and adventure travel hub, especially the intricate cluster of mountains that resides at the centre of the peninsula. Rising to a height of over 2,400 m (7,900 ft), the mountains of the Mani region are ripe with opportunities for climbing, camping and trekking, while the Alfios River is ideal for whitewater rafting and kayaking.

The peninsula is also the home of the famous Kalamata olive, which takes its name from Kalamata, the second largest city in south Peloponnese. When preserved and eaten whole, the large black olives are rich and have an almost meaty texture; both black and green olives are also pressed into a fine extra virgin olive oil which is exported worldwide. Other local treats include rose-petal jam and cured pork. Meanwhile, the northern Peloponnese area is regaining appreciation among wine connoisseurs for its red vintages and ambrosial white dessert wines that complement Greek cuisine.

corinth and mycenae

Nearly everyone who visits the Peloponnese arrives via the narrow Isthmus of Corinth, which separates the peninsula from the Greek mainland. The isthmus is dissected by the man-made Corinth Canal, one of the wonders of 19th-century engineering. Completed in 1893, the canal is only 21 m (69 ft) wide. Although too narrow for many modern cargo ships, it remains a popular maritime route between the Aegean and the central Mediterranean.

Both landmarks take their name from nearby Ancient Corinth and its acropolis the Acrocorinth, where the Temple of Aphrodite resides. One of Greece's most impressive cities of antiquity, Corinth became a rich city-state under Roman rule in 146 BC. Flush with wealth, the population grew to nearly a million people. The ancient city was also reputed for its decadence. Its inhabitants were known to have watched mock sea battles in the giant amphitheatre, shopped in the sprawling Agora, worshipped at the stunning Temple of Apollo and partied to such an extent that St Paul condemned them in his gospels.

After the original Corinth was destroyed by an earthquake in the 1850s, a new version of the city arose on the nearby coastal plain. Located at the junction of the eponymous isthmus, canal and gulf, modern Corinth is a natural transportation hub as well as an industrial centre

THIS PAGE: *A modern restaging of an ancient ritual at Olympia, in which a high priestess ignites a flame prior to the Olympics.*
PAGE 76: *The narrow Corinth Canal divides the Peloponnese from mainland Greece.*

THIS PAGE: *Looking down from the Palamidi fortress on the Acronafplia, one has a lovely view of the old town and Nafplion's picturesque harbour.*

OPPOSITE (FROM TOP): *Nafplion is renowned for its vibrant arts scene and music festival; a scene from the movie 300 is transformed into a giant canvas and displayed at the ruins of ancient Sparta.*

of no small repute, known for its petrochemicals, food processing and construction materials. When the *Proastiakós* (suburban) light rail network linked the city directly to Athens in 2005, commuting between Corinth and the capital became more convenient, a factor that will no doubt spark even greater growth in years to come.

South of Corinth is another treasure of Greek archaeology—the ruins of ancient Mycenae. This fortified hill town was one of the fulcrums of Greek civilisation, whose origins are closely linked to the mythical Perseus, the son of Zeus and Danaë. Evidence of sprawling palace ruins suggest that Mycenae was a powerful kingdom during its time, whose rule spanned four centuries. However, with its demise in 1100 BC, the settlement lay forgotten in history and was only rediscovered in 1874 by the noted German archaeologist Heinrich Schliemann. Excavations have uncovered a royal palace, ceremonial gateway and various tombs from which gold was unearthed.

nafplion

With a population of around 16,000, Nafplion thrives as both a seaport and weekend getaway from Athens. The red-roofed town didn't rise to prominence until the Middle Ages, when the Venetians transformed it from a sleepy fishing village into a trade entrepôt protected by the massive Acronafplia and Palamidi fortresses, which lie on a rocky ridge overlooking the harbour. In 1829, the city became the first capital of independent, modern Greece. While Nafplion didn't hang on to the reins of power for very long, much of the city's character dates from that era, in particular the neoclassical mansions and public buildings of the old town.

Although nearby Argos was an ancient city-state, Nafplion is a relative latecomer in the annals of Greek history. As a result, locals tend to pride themselves in more recent events, in particular the early 19th-century Greek struggle for independence, when the town became an epicentre for both homegrown patriots and enthusiastic 'philhellenes' from overseas who gave their time, money and even lives towards the cause of Greek freedom. Among the latter was British poet Lord Byron, who died from a fever contracted during the Ottomans' siege of Messolonghi, and is among those immortalised at the Catholic Church of the Metamorphosis (Potamianou Street).

Today, Nafplion remains a city of thinkers and intellectuals, the hometown of many famous writers, and the location of one of the nation's most distinguished learning centres, the University of Peloponnese School of Fine Arts, renowned for theatre, dance and stage design. Named after the son of Poseidon, the city still retains its intimate relationship with the sea; its port shelters fishing boats and a fleet of mega yachts, and boasts a picturesque harbour. The charming ambience and thriving cultural scene have long attracted foreigners to Nafplion—some stay for a season, others stay far longer than that. As a result, the town is imbued with a cosmopolitanism that is seldom found in other Greek cities of this size.

Syntagma Square is a charming place to sit and simply watch the world pass by, or indulge in a long afternoon of window shopping. Much of the city's best shopping is found just a short stroll from the leafy square, with boutiques selling locally-designed jewellery and clothing, while trinkets such as worry beads, amulets, textiles and ceramics also abound.

land of the spartans

Spartans are all the rage these days, in the wake of the film *300* and Frank Miller's graphic novel of the same name—which makes it all the more disappointing that there isn't much left of ancient Sparta (Spárti), thanks to centuries of pilfering. The bulk of the ruins and museum pieces are actually Roman. Nearby, Mistra offers more links to Greek history—the fortified town flourished from the 13th to 15th centuries as one of the last outposts of classic Byzantine civilisation.

The southern Peloponnese is probably the most picturesque part of the entire peninsula, especially because of its stark, awe-inspiring landscapes. Monemvasía well deserves its moniker as the 'Gibraltar of Greece'—it is a medieval fortified town perched beneath a sheer 350-m (1,150-ft)-tall mountain, on an island connected to the mainland by only a narrow causeway.

Its name is particularly fitting, as it translates to 'single entrance' in Greek. Even more stunning is the remote and rugged Mani peninsula, with its deep ravines and towering peaks. Mount Taygetos, where the Spartans once executed their criminals and abandoned 'unfit' children to fend for themselves, is now a major trekking destination. Inner Mani—geographically the outer part of the peninsula—is known for its ancient churches and stone tower houses. During summer, the region suffers from punishing temperatures. The heat is so extreme that ancient Greeks believed that Mani was the gateway to Hades. For that same reason, trekking through the mountain range is best done during the cooler months, particularly in spring when the hillsides are bathed in wildflowers.

olympia and patras

Around the west of the Peloponnese are the ruins of Olympia, an athletics venue and a religious centre which thrived for more than a thousand years, from the Mycenaean through Roman times. It was dedicated to the Greek god Zeus, ruler of Mount Olympus. Held every four years between 776 BC and 393 AD, the Olympics were originally created to honour the Greek god. While competition was no doubt paramount, the ancient games always had spiritual overtones. Banned in 394 AD due to its pagan origins, the athletic event only returned to Greece in 1896, with the first modern Olympics staged in Athens instead of its original home. However, during the 2004 Athens Games, various track and field events were staged at Olympia. Hordes of tourists descended as interest in the ancient site surged anew; however, the city still manages to maintain its original character. Ancient Olympia, in particular, retains its aura of grandeur with the multi-columned Palaestra—many wrestlers trained here prior to the games—and there is an impressive stadium and a collection of temples set within its idyllic, verdant surrounds.

Patras is the nation's third largest city, with a population of 230,000. The hardworking seaport and university town can't compare with the antiquities of Ancient Olympia but it has its share of Venetian castles and ruins. Patras boasts a thriving nightlife and arts scene—being the 'European Cultural Capital' in 2006—and Greece's biggest bash, the annual Patras Carnival. Beginning in mid January on Aghios Andreas, Saint Andrew's Day—the Patron Saint of Patras—the festival continues for weeks. Festivities include *Tsiknopempti,* Smokey Thursday—marking the last day Orthodox Christians eat meat before fasting for 40 days until Greek Easter; the Carnival Parade with over 50,000 participants; and the grand finale where an effigy of the carnival king is burned in a giant bonfire along the waterfront, followed by a spectacular fireworks display.

Rio is a charming seaside destination with summer villas, enticing nightlife and alluring coastal views. On a cloudless day, one can clearly see the world's longest suspension bridge, the Rio-Antirrio Bridge, connecting the Peloponnese to the Greek mainland.

THIS PAGE: Spring brings a profusion of wildflowers to the Peloponnese countryside.

OPPOSITE: An engineering feat, the 2880-m- (9449-ft-) long Rio-Antirrio Bridge links Patras to the mainland.

Ancient Olympia, in particular, retains its aura of grandeur...

nafplia palace hotel + villas

With its great store of culture and numerous historical ruins, the Peloponnese peninsula presents a unique perspective on Greek life that reaches far beyond the walls of Athens. It encompasses modern cities such as Kalamata and Corinth alongside fortress towns, temples, ancient healing centres built atop mineral springs, and famous historical sites such as Olympia—the original home of the Olympic Games. It's no wonder that the region has maintained its allure among holidaymakers for much of the last century.

It is here along the coast that one finds the intimate city of Nafplion. Although it was made the first capital of modern Greece in 1823, the Nafplion of today enjoys a more modest population than its neighbouring cities. A sense of peace permeates its airy streets, all the better for one to take in the multifarious architectural influences that have left their mark over the years. Byzantine

and Roman structures stand with relics of the Venetian and Ottoman empires throughout the picturesque squares.

Through all this, the Nafplia Palace lies perfectly at ease with the surroundings. Indeed, it is hard to tell where the seams between past and present are located. From its position high above the city and the Bay of Argolis, the five-star resort hotel occupies an ancient Venetian stronghold on the site of the Nafplion Acropolis which dates back to the Bronze Age. Designed by renowned architects T Papayannis & Associates and G Fatseas, Lighting, the palace is nothing less than a masterpiece. With its form so perfectly married to the spirit of its surroundings, the landscape can no longer be imagined without the Nafplia Palace upon it, and vice versa.

Within its generous limits, the hotel offers 51 luxurious guestrooms and 33 villas built upon the slopes for an advantageous

THIS PAGE (FROM TOP): *Nafplia Palace blends with the surrounding natural and historic landscape; picture windows invite sunlight and allow views of the sea.*

OPPOSITE (FROM LEFT): *Enjoy a spa experience in your own room; the hotel's décor of rough-hewn stone blends perfectly with the Venetian ruins that it occupies.*

view of the castle and waters to the south. Various room configurations are available, and to simplify choices the hotel has created four distinct categories to suit a range of needs. Regardless of whether one prefers Comfort Club, Exclusive Club, Premium Club, or Platinum Club accommodations modern amenities such as air-conditioning, minibars, and business-friendly communications come as standard features. All room interiors are carefully constructed to achieve a subtle warmth and a feeling of quality, right down to the marble bathrooms with their range of Bulgari toiletries.

Many of the Exclusive Club villas feature their own private pools, while Premium Club suites and villas up the residential quotient with separate living areas, multiple terraces, and enhanced sea views. The Palace Villa Sea View is the crown of the Platinum Club level, with two sumptuous bedrooms and a large

10-m (33-ft) pool on a private marble terrace. Both rooms enjoy en-suite bathrooms with hydromassage tubs, steam baths and shower cabins for a spa-like pampering experience. The villa also boasts a kitchenette, its own screening room with Dolby surround sound, and three plasma televisions throughout the property and dining area.

Guests can call for an intimate meal in privacy on their own balcony, but if that sounds a little too removed from the action, dining out at any of the 10 restaurants and bars on and near the property is guaranteed to be as exhilarating as the views. From fine Italian dining at Amimoni, to the relaxed al fresco atmosphere of Kafenion, the Nafplia Palace's interpretation of Mediterranean life is always colourful and wholly authentic. Here in a place where the ancient is made new again, there are always refreshing ways to discover the meaning of Greek hospitality.

rooms
51 rooms and suites • 33 villas

food
Amimoni: Italian fine dining • Kafenion: salads, grills and drinks • Ilios: all-day dining • Arvanitia Beach Bar & Restaurant: casual seaside dining

drink
Veranda Bar: lounge bar • Pool Bar

features
spa and beauty centre • infinity pool for villa guests • helipad • florist • room service • wireless Internet access

nearby
Nafplion • beach • Palamidi Fortress • Bourtzi island fortress • Argos • Mycenae

contact
Akronafplia, 21100 Nafplion, Peloponnese • telephone: +30.275.207 0800 • facsimile: +30.275.202 8783 • email: reservations@nafplionhotels.gr • website: www.nafplionhotels.gr

centralgreece

BULGARIA

TURKEY

FORMER YUGOSLAV
REPUBLIC
OF MACEDONIA

EAST MACEDONIA, THRACE

Sea
Marm

TURKEY

CENTRAL MACEDONIA

Thasos

Samothraki

ALBANIA

Kosani

Limnos

WEST
MACEDONIA

▲ Mount Olympus

North Aegean Islands

Lesvos

Larisa

Ioannina

Trikala

THESSALY

Volos

Northern Sporades

EPIRUS

Skyros

Lamia

Antipsara

Paxoi

Chios

EUBOEA

⟩ Estate Hatzimichalis

Aegean Sea

Lefkada

Ionian Islands

WESTERN GREECE

MAINLAND
GREECE

Chalkida

Samos

Delphi

▲ Mount
Parnassus

Messolonghi

ATTICA

Andros

Ithaca

Gulf of Corinth

Ikaria

Cephalonia

Kea

Tinos

Zakynthos

Kythnos

Syros

Naxos

PELOPONNESE

Serifos

Paros

Amorgos

Hydra

Sifnos

Sikinos

Ios

Milos

Santorini

Anafi

Mediterranean Sea

The Cyclades

Legend

Highway

Main Roa

Lak

Urban Are

2000–3000 r

1500–2000 r

1000–1500 r

500–1000 r

200–500 r

100–200 r

Sea of Crete

0 km   25   50   75 k

Kythira

central greece

North of the Attica peninsula, the mainland widens into an expansive landscape stretching from sea to sea—a section of rugged mountains, deep ravines, fertile valleys and coastlands that are still refreshingly undeveloped. Being geographically close to the Balkans also means that central Greece stands out in terms of its culture. A historic crossroads of different traditions, ethnicities and languages that was also under Ottoman rule for almost a century even after Hellenic independence, it is no surprise that central Greece has been endowed with a more eastern, exotic patina than the rest of the country.

Central Greece comprises three distinct regions: Thessaly in the east along the Aegean; mainland Greece in the south along the Gulf of Corinth; and Epirus in the west along the Ionian coast. While far less of a tourist hotspot than Athens and the islands, the middle of the country does have its special attractions with its pristine beaches and famous battlefields, ancient ruins and Orthodox monasteries. Rocky outcrops and pine-forested mountains add to the region's allure, and create ample opportunity for adventure sports such as rock climbing, whitewater rafting, mountain biking, skiing, snowboarding, paragliding and bouldering.

playground of the gods

Although the grandest and most celebrated temples and churches were erected in Athens and other major cities, in many respects, central Greece remains the nation's religious heartland. Much of Greek mythology unfolds in the mountains, forests and caves of this region. This was also home to the Oracle of Delphi and the scene of the religion-inspired Sacred Wars that plagued Greece during 6th century BC.

One of the most storied places in the Mediterranean, Delphi was a place of spiritual pilgrimage for more than a millennium. The ancients believed that the summit of Mount Parnassus was the home of Apollo, and they would trek to the lofty shrine to pay homage to the god of healing and prophecy and pray for good health or a vision of their future. The famed Oracle—a senior female priestess—was the medium through which Apollo delivered his missives. Today, Delphi is a modern town and a UNESCO World Heritage Site. The well-preserved ruins include the sublime Temple of Apollo, as well as an amphitheatre, treasury and a circular *tholos* structure; many of the marble and metal artefacts discovered at Delphi are on display at the site museum.

Whether it was due to its sacred roots or the region's rugged topography, central Greece endured as a spiritual hub for several thousand years, even during the dark days of the Ottoman occupation. Mountainous retreats such as Meteora and Hosios Loukas enabled Greek Orthodox monks to escape both their Muslim overseers and the temptations of the secular world, preserving not only their deep faith but also Byzantine art and architecture. Although the 21st

THIS PAGE: The mountainous terrain of central Greece challenges even the most skilled rock climbers.

PAGE 86: Orthodox monasteries such as this were built high up in the rocky outcrop of Meteora to escape from the Ottomans.

century made its presence strongly felt during the 2004 Olympics, much of the region remains lost in time. Traditional Greece thrives with its plethora of cobblestoned villages and farms, with natives who would most likely list their occupation as farmer or fisherman rather than banker or businessman. A world away from the crowded beaches often associated with cosmopolitan Greece, the central region offers an unadulterated insight into native Greek lifestyle.

sand, sea and snow

On the far side of the mountains from Delphi is the Fthiotida Coast. Popular with local vacationers for its hot springs, this natural spa location is virtually unknown to foreigners, who usually limit themselves to the Greek islands when looking for a seaside sojourn. Athenians flock to this coast on weekends and during the August holidays, as it tends to be less crowded than other destinations. It is also easy to reach via the Athens-Lamía motorway that runs from the city straight to the coast. Despite its proximity to the sea, Fthiotida is primarily mountainous, with ancient footpaths that lead the intrepid traveller to unhindered panoramas. The area also boasts a myriad of local culinary delights, including *myzithra* cheese, *kourambiedes* almond cookies and *trachana* dumplings.

THIS PAGE (FROM TOP): A light dusting of snow blankets lemons after a winter storm blows across central Greece; the Moutzouris steam train makes its way between Ano Lehonia and Milies on the Pelion peninsula.

OPPOSITE: An aerial view of the ancient Roman city of Nikopolis, founded by Octavian to commemorate his victory over Antony and Cleopatra at nearby Actium.

Adding to its appeal to outdoor sports enthusiasts, Fthiotida is one of the few places in Greece that offers the alluring possibility of experiencing sand, sea and snow in a single day. Brilliant white-sand beaches such as Livanates are only a short drive from the slopes of the 2,450-m (8,000-ft)-tall Mount Parnassus. The snow season lasts only from December to April, but the mountain is home to the Parnassos Ski Centre, Greece's largest venue for skiing and snow sports. Anyone who makes light of the skiing opportunities in Greece should consider the fact that the International Ski Federation (FIS) schedules regular slalom, giant slalom and snowboard events on this peak; points earned here count towards the world championships. Although trendy young Athenians dominate the area, the winter party scene is a cosmopolitan one, especially in the mountainside village of Aráhova with its crowded tavernas, bars and music clubs.

Surrounded by olive groves and vineyards, Atalanti is the agricultural hub of the Fthiotis prefecture, and the home of several prominent winemakers, whose artisanal vintages have taken the world by storm. Also on the coastal strip between Mount Parnassus and the Euboean Gulf are a number of sandy beaches and the charming town of Aghios Konstantinos, a main ferry port from which to access the nearby Sporades Islands.

The region is not without ties to ancient myths and genuine history. Thebes, the second largest city of the Boeotia prefecture, was the legendary birthplace of Hercules as well as the city-state ruled by the tragic Oedipus of Greek drama. The narrow pass at Thermopylae is where the Greek army, led by King Leonidas and his 300 Spartans, made their heroic stand against the Persians in 480 BC. As a tribute to the Spartan King's bravery, the once bloody battlefield is now marked by an imposing statue of the Spartan commander next to a burial mound.

thessaly

The fertile plains of Thessaly (Thessalia) make up one of Greece's most important bread baskets. Passing through the region, one is greeted by a golden expanse of wheat, corn and barley set against a dramatic backdrop of distant mountains. Dynamic cities such as Larisa and Volos dominate the region's business scene. At first glance, they may not appear to have much to lure one off the highway, but they do have their special charms, such as the waterfront *ouzeri* taverns of Volos—said to be the country's best. While many people travel through Thessaly on the busy motorway and railway line that connect Athens with the rest of Europe, few linger in the agricultural heartland—save on the fringes, such as the heavily wooded Pelion peninsula in the east and the craggy mountains that define the province's northern border.

The hook-shaped Pelion peninsula curves between the mainland and Sporades islands, creating the broad Pagasetic Gulf. The terrain is extremely mountainous and largely covered in orchards and native forest. Ancient cobblestone donkey trails called *kalderímia* meander through sprawling forests of maple, oak, beech and chestnut trees, creating a path that connects the peninsula's many mountain villages and secluded beaches. Popular with hiking enthusiasts, the area is also rich in wildlife, especially birds and butterflies.

The Pelion featured prominently in Greek mythology as the homeland of the mischievous centaurs, rowdy mythical beings said to have the head and torso of a man, and the body and legs of a horse. Jason and the Argonauts were also known to depart from Volos (ancient Iolkós), to begin their journey of acquiring the Golden Fleece. In much more recent days, the coastal city served as a secure hiding place for Jews during the Nazi occupation.

At the northern extreme of Thessaly is the traditional divide between northern and central Greece—the towering Mount Olympus, traditional abode of the gods and the place from which Zeus ruled over heaven and earth. Ancient Greeks believed that the clouds which often swathed the mountain were a gate through which only the divine could pass, and that the summit was crowned by a magnificent palace in which Zeus and the Olympian gods whiled away their days drinking ambrosia as they toyed with the fate of mortals. Today, the summit can be reached via walking paths from the quaint Litóchoro village.

epirus and the far north

Few make it as far as Epirus, the province wedged between the Pindos mountain range, Albania and the Ionian Sea. But for those who do, secluded beaches, picturesque 19th-century villages, distinctive regional cuisine and a charmingly slow pace of life await. Given its strategic position at the bottom of the Balkans—and the number of different people who have ruled it over the years—it's unsurprising that the culture of Epirus is such an eclectic mix. Left behind in the rush for independence, Epirus remained under Ottoman hands until 1913. Traces of the exotic east still exist, as well as a fierce self-sufficiency inculcated from centuries of Epirotes having to fend for themselves.

With its distinctive minaret and domed mosque, Ioannina still carries a certain Ottoman air and memories of the days when it was the stronghold of Ali Pasha. An 18th-century Muslim administrator initially appointed by the Ottomans, the brutal and brilliant warlord of Turkish-Albanian descent allied himself with local Christians and transformed Epirus into a small private kingdom with himself as monarch. Lord Byron himself came to visit Ali Pasha in 1809, a meeting immortalised in his poem, *Childe Harold's Pilgrimage*. These days, the Epirote capital is known for its burgeoning cultural scene, gourmet restaurants and vibrant university student community. Long hidden away by the impassive Pindos mountain range, the completion of the Via Egnatia highway is sure to attract more international attention.

Down the Ionian coast, the romantic little beach resort of Párga resembles a miniature Dubrovnik, with its red-tiled roofs scattered around a horseshoe-shaped bay. In the northeast, the isolated villages of Zagoria reveal Epirus' natural splendour. Part of the Pindos Mountains, the area largely escaped foreign occupation due to its inaccessibility, and Zagoria's flourishing temperate ecosystem and rich Byzantium heritage reveal Hellenic culture at its purest.

THIS PAGE: *Fetiche Pasha Mosque, housed inside the Castle of Ioannina, was originally a Byzantine stronghold. It later became an Ottoman lair.*

OPPOSITE: *Seen from an ancient footbridge, the dramatic Vikos Gorge epitomises the natural magnificence of Zagoria.*

...Hellenic culture at its purest.

estate hatzimichalis

THIS PAGE (FROM TOP): *Estate Hatzimichalis is located in the shadow of Mount Parnassus; every vineyard in the estate occupies a unique terroir.*

OPPOSITE (FROM LEFT): *The estate's cool cellars hold more than 2,500 French oak barrels; Estate Hatzimichalis wines are renowned the world over.*

It's poetically fitting that Estate Hatzimichalis should prosper in the shadow of Mount Parnassus. For what better place to grow grapes—and transform them into marvellous wine—than near the snow-capped peak that was sacred to Dionysus, the ancient Greek god of both wine and pleasure.

Owner Dimitris Hatzimichalis began planting grape vines on newly acquired land around the town of Atalanti in 1973. Aiming to produce wines different from—and better than—what was already available in the area, he started experimenting with indigenous varieties and researching ancient grape types.

With his daring experimental vineyards, Hatzimichalis was the first of the new wave of Greek winemakers to break the monopoly of the four or five large companies that previously held the domestic market in a tight grip. By the mid 1980s, he had become a household name in Greece, and built a solid reputation overseas with his premium wines.

From its initial 9 hectares (22 acres), the Hatzimichalis vineyards have grown over the years to more than 220 hectares (544 acres) in total. Among the many varieties cultivated on the estate are reds such as Cabernet Sauvignon, Cabernet Franc, Merlot, Syrah, Carignan, Xynomavro and Limnio, and whites like Chardonnay, Robola, Athiri, Assyrtiko and Sauvignon Blanc. Every vineyard is grown in an individual terroir, where factors such as land and soil have been taken into careful consideration, resulting in rich, individual wines which reflect their terroirs' microclimate.

Hatzimichalis' success is even more surprising given the fact that his professional background lay in the import and manufacture

products
wines · books · accessories · souvenirs

food
restaurant: traditional Greek

recommendations
Kapnias White · Raches Galanou Red · Merlot · Cabernet Sauvignon Late Release · Cava LX

features
guided tours · wine tastings · historical exhibits · store

nearby
Atalanti town · Atalanti Museum · Mount Parnassus · Delphi archaeological site and museum · archaeological sites · ski lodge

contact
Estate Hatzimichalis, c/o Demeter S A
13th km Athens-Lamia National Road
14564 Nea Kifisia
telephone: +30.210.807 6705 ·
facsimile: +30.210.807 6704 ·
email: info@hatzimichalis.gr ·
website: www.hatzimichalis.gr

of electronic goods rather than in vine-growing or winemaking. Innovative and forward-thinking, Dimitris Hatzimichalis realised that the cool downdrafts from Mount Parnassus would keep summer temperatures from rising too high, while the sea breeze from the Euboean Gulf would keep winter frost at bay—a perfect combination for producing premium wine grapes.

Located near Atalanti town, the estate's integrated winemaking facility comprises vineyards, a winery, a bottling plant, and climate-controlled cellars for wine aging, which hold more than 2,500 French oak barrels with a capacity of 228 l (60 gal) each. The visitors' centre has a tasting area and restaurant. There is also a shop that sells wine, along with accessories, souvenirs and books; among the books are several penned by Dimitris Hatzimichalis on the history of winemaking.

The entire winery is a living museum where the past—exhibitions about the Greek winemaking tradition—and the present—state-of-the-art wine production—come together. Tours of the estate include a visit to the exhibition vineyard, production facilities and underground cellars, while informative displays introduce the history of corks, bottles and barrels, wine transportation and storage over the centuries, 19th-century winemaking tools, and the various shapes that bottle openers have taken through the ages.

Bicycle rides or walks through the vineyards can be arranged, and an open theatre is also available for artistic and educational activities. A multi-purpose hall with high-tech audiovisual equipment can be rented for conferences and seminars for about 150 people. Last but not least, the property also boasts a chapel for weddings and other special events.

northerngreece

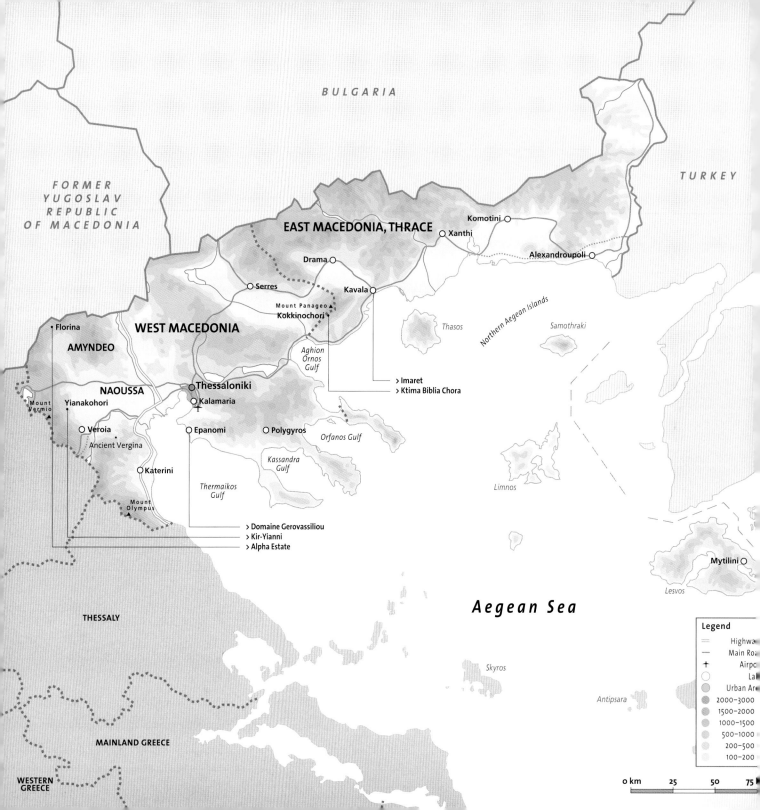

BULGARIA

FORMER
YUGOSLAV
REPUBLIC
OF MACEDONIA

TURKEY

EAST MACEDONIA, THRACE

Komotini ○

Xanthi ○

Alexandroupoli ○

Drama ○

Serres ○

Kavala ○

Mount Panageo ▲
Kokkinochori

WEST MACEDONIA

Thasos

Northern Aegean Islands

Samothraki

AMYNDEO

Florina •

Aghion Örnos Gulf

> Imaret
> Ktima Biblia Chora

NAOUSSA

Thessaloniki ○

Yianakohori •

Kalamaria

Mount
Vermio ▲

Epanomi ○

Polygyros ○

Orfanos Gulf

Veroia ○

Ancient Vergina •

*Kassandra
Gulf*

Limnos

Katerini ○

*Thermaikos
Gulf*

Mount
Olympus ▲

> Domaine Gerovassiliou
> Kir-Yianni
> Alpha Estate

Mytilini ○

Lesvos

THESSALY

Aegean Sea

Skyros

Antipsara

MAINLAND GREECE

WESTERN
GREECE

Legend	
═══	Highwa
───	Main Ro
✛	Airpo
○	La
	Urban Ar
	2000–3000
	1500–2000
	1000–1500
	500–1000
	200–500
	100–200

0 km   25   50   75

northern greece

Even more than the rest of the nation, northern Greece is a crossroad of world history and culture. As a strategic stepping stone between southern Europe and western Asia, the region has witnessed the march of innumerable armies over the last 3,000 years, from troops led by legendary figures such as Alexander the Great as well as the invading forces of the Persians, Romans, Visigoths, Huns, Byzantines and Ottomans.

Spanning roughly 600 km (400 miles) from east to west, the region is generally divided into three broad areas: Thrace in the east, Macedonia in the middle and the Pindos mountain range in the west. Although northern Greece has quite a considerable coastline—thanks in no small part to the three-armed Chalkidiki peninsula—the region often feels more like the Balkans than the Mediterranean. For one thing, the climate is different, with cooler winters and more precipitation than its southern counterparts. This contributes to diverse flora and wildlife that thrive on wetter ecosystems. Being so far north, even the crops are different—broad river valleys filled with tobacco, fruit orchards, vineyards and amber waves of grain.

Earlier waves of tourism tended to bypass the north, leaving it largely untouched by modern lifestyles. In recent years, however, the region has become a popular destination for those seeking to explore an older, quieter and more traditional side of Greece.

THIS PAGE (FROM TOP): Many flock to Thessaloniki for the annual international film festival; a statue of Macedonian icon Alexander the Great.

PAGE 96: Aghios Therapon Church towers over the waterfront of Mytilini, Lesvos.

thessaloniki

Often called Greece's 'second capital' because of its considerable political clout and economic muscle, Thessaloniki harbours a population of roughly one million people. The city's urban area sprawls along the northern shore of the Thermaic Gulf, a thriving port and an important highway and railway hub with connections throughout the Balkans. From oil and steel to textiles and machinery, Thessaloniki has always been a hardworking cousin to Athens. In recent years, however, the manufacturing industry has started to decline, replaced by modern trade, commerce and epicurean industries such as wine production. The city's cultural significance is also quite considerable. It plays host to such events as the annual International Thessaloniki Film Festival—one of the most important film festivals in Europe that showcases the works of upcoming directors, the Dimitria Folklore Festival and various sporting events. A star among Balkan cities, Thessaloniki was named the 'European Capital of Culture' in 1997.

Thessalonians are justifiably proud of their city...

Thessalonians are justifiably proud of their city, and often boast that their hometown has contributed more to modern culture than any other city, including Athens. This hardly comes as a surprise with the city annually hosting Greece's various trade conventions. One of the larger events, Thessaloniki International Trade Fair, showcases the newest developments in commercial trade, ranging from *avant garde* fashion and interior design, to cutting-edge gadgetry and the latest fads in eco-culture. The city's constant fascination with all things modern has not only gained for itself recogintion on the global stage as a key player in defining commercial trends, it has also successfully aided in rebranding Greece from a living museum into a dynamic, regional economic hub.

Founded in 315 BC, Thessaloniki later became the capital of the Roman province of Macedonia and a distinguished Byzantine metropolis. Both of those periods endowed 'Salonika'—as it was called then—with a wealth of Byzantine architecture. The modern-day Dimitriou Gounari pedestrian street runs through the heart of what was once the Roman city, connecting the Arch of Galerius—an ancient monument with elaborate marble panels dedicated to the glory of Roman emperor Galerius—with other classical icons such as the Rotunda, one of the oldest Christian churches in the world, and excavations of the Roman palace. The historical stone monuments offer a striking visual foil to the modern high-rise buildings and trendy fashion boutiques that flank the city's most stylish street.

Farther west are great Byzantine churches such as the 8th-century Aghia Sophia (based on its predecessor the Hagia Sophia in Istanbul), and the Aghios Dimitrios—both of which are UNESCO World Heritage Sites. Although the latter was all but destroyed in the Great Fire of 1917 and took decades to restore, it is now one of the largest churches in Greece. The superb Archaeological Museum safeguards many of the city's ancient Greek and Roman treasures, while the adjacent Museum of Byzantine Culture details local Greek culture from 500 AD through Ottoman times.

Thessaloniki isn't content to simply rest on its ancient laurels. It's also a thoroughly modern city with exuberent nightlife. Sidewalk cafés line the waterfront Aristotélous Square, while the olive oil warehouses of the Ladadika district have been converted into nightclubs, coffee bars and gourmet restaurants. In addition to its role as one of the city's commercial districts, Ladadika was once the heart of the city's thriving Jewish quarter—one of the largest in the Balkans—until the Holocaust, when an estimated 96 percent of the local Jewish community perished. Much of the old Turkish bazaar has also been refurbished into a modern shopping hub, especially the domed Bezesteni, where one can purchase Oriental carpets and exotic golden jewellery.

In keeping with Thessalonki's status as one of Europe's cultural capitals, there are a number of ways to soak up the local arts vibe. One of the more popular venues is the lively Mylos, a hip nightlife complex that occupies a converted flour mill and features music, comedy and art

THIS PAGE (FROM TOP): People often play racquetball and other such sports on the many beaches near Thessaloniki; remains of a Roman aqueduct on the island of Lesvos.

OPPOSITE: One of the largest churches in Greece, the Aghios Dimitrios of Thessaloniki was rebuilt after a devastating fire in the early 20th century.

exhibitions. Large-scale events such as the Thessaloniki Biennale are also breaking new ground in the European art scene with their showcase on contemporary Eastern European art. It has helped to generate an irreverent vibe that is fast beginning to outshine its antiquity-filled competition, Athens.

epanomi and the chalkidiki

Along the eastern shore of the gulf lies the photogenic seaside town of Epanomi. The second-oldest settlement in northern Greece—the oldest being Aggelohori—the area has been occupied since the Neolithic era. However, it was only in recent years that Epanomi gained any sort of recognition outside the immediate region, thanks to the establishment of high-class resort facilities and a modern wine industry. Thessalonians flock here on weekends for the pristine beaches, fresh seafood and a local grape liqueur called *tsipouro* that packs quite a punch. The area is also gaining a reputation for its production of fine wine, being home to vintners such as Domaine Gerovassiliou, which doubles as a tourist attraction in its own right—Domaine Gerovassiliou welcomes visitors to its cellar and hosts a small wine museum with displays of antique bottles, wine presses and corkscrews.

THIS PAGE: A cultural hub in its own right, Thessaloniki hosted its first Biennial of Contemporary Art in 2007.

OPPOSITE: Visitors are required to obtain special permission before they may visit the 20 monasteries of Mount Athos and only men are allowed to enter the area.

Epanomi is also a gateway to the wondrous Chalkidiki peninsula, a timeless landscape of olive groves, pine forest and rocky coastlines where modern life still seems very far away. The region's Petrálona Caves are where the oldest human remains in all of Greece were found, and the hilltop village of Stágeira lies just a few kilometres from the ancient city of the same name, where the philosopher Aristotle was born in 384 BC.

Further down the peninsula is the sacred Mount Athos, home to 20 Greek Orthodox monasteries and more than 1,700 black-clad and long-bearded monks. For nearly a thousand years (since 1060 AD), females have been banned from setting foot on the Athos peninsula—and that goes for females of any species (only cats and chickens are exempt from this rule; the former are kept for rodent hunting, and the latter for its eggs which the monks use to create the paint used for their artworks). Although the peninsula is land-linked, access is only possible via water, and visitors are required to obtain a special pass before they are permitted to visit the monasteries. In order to preserve its unique status, the national government transformed the peninsula into the Theocratic Republic of Athos in 1926, a self-governing, semi-independent state ruled by these Orthodox monks.

the macedonian heartland

Due west of Thessaloniki is an area of river valleys and rolling hills where the ancient Macedonian civilisation was born. According to legend, migrants from the Greek city of Argos founded the civilisation around 800 BC. But it wasn't until the middle of the 4th century BC that Macedonia emerged as a regional power under the ambitious Philip II. It was Philip's son—the incomparable Alexander the Great—who extended Macedonian rule over the whole of the peninsula and then Hellenic rule all the way from the Mediterranean to as far as India.

Philip built his capital at Pella, now the most important archaeological site in all of northern Greece and a major tourist attraction. Although most of the buildings crumbled to ruin long ago, many of the city's stunning mosaic murals have withstood the test of time and are preserved at the Pella Museum. More Macedonian relics can be found at nearby Lefkádia, where four tombs have mosaics depicting scenes of ancient life and legends.

The riverside village of Naoussa provides a tranquil retreat between the ruins, with waterfront cafés serving fresh fish and superb wine from well-known local vineyards. More fine grapes and vintages can be found on the nearby Amyndeon plateau, which houses a mix of vineyards, whitewashed farmhouses and the deep blue Lake Vegoritida, which, along with the nearby Préspa Lakes, is an important sanctuary for migratory birds. This region is known for producing some of the best wines in Greece, if not the entire Mediterranean.

kavala and the turkish frontier

Straddling the busy coastal route between Thessaloniki and Istanbul is the city of Kavala, with its eclectic blend of Greek and Turkish qualities. Part of the Ottoman Empire for more than 500 years—and located close to the imperial capital—the city could hardly avoid Turkish influence. In fact, the sultans of the time poured considerable funds into local infrastructure. Kavala also benefited from the thousands of enterprising Greek refugees who relocated here from Asia Minor after the Greco-Turkish War of 1919–1922.

With its fishing boats, yachts and tavernas, Kavala's harbour presents a quintessentially Greek image. However, the city's architectural icon is the aqueduct with its 60 soaring arches. Commissioned by Suleiman the Magnificent, the aqueduct is a relic from the city's days under Ottoman rule. Kavala's most famous 'native son' is Mehmet Ali (1769–1849), a local of Albanian heritage who would later become Mohamed Ali Pasha, the most powerful sultan of Egypt. Ali's birthplace is still a local landmark. The Panagia (Old Town) is Kavala's most historic neighbourhood—a warren of cobblestone lanes and tightly packed houses that crowd together on a peninsula extending into the harbour. In the midst is a cluster of old Ottoman-era buildings called the Imaret, fully refurbished to house a boutique hotel, restaurant and spa, with stunning views across the bay and town.

The coastal mountains west of Kavala constitute one of the more picturesque areas of the panhandle and also one of the cradles of Greek wine. Estates such as Ktima Biblia Chora continue the viticultural tradition established by Phoenician settlers over 3,000 years ago.

East of Kavala lies Thrace, an ancient province that even native Greeks have little knowledge of. Wedged between Bulgaria and the northern Aegean, this sliver of land has seen its fair share of action, being constantly transferred between various rulers and empires over the ages. Contemporary Thrace is set apart from the rest of Greece due to its unique status as the home of the country's largest Muslim population—a flourishing minority that continue to cling on to their faith and traditions today.

The region's economy remains largely dependent on agriculture and maritime ventures, although tourism is slowly making inroads into this far-flung hinterland. The recent completion of the Via Egnatia Highway—which follows the route of an ancient Roman road across northern Greece—has created a miniature economic boom here and made Thrace's flourishing woodlands much more accessible to those travelling from Thessaloniki and Istanbul.

THIS PAGE: Despite its sleek Roman lines, the aqueduct in Kavala was actually built during the Ottoman period.

OPPOSITE: Kavala's rich history and seaside charm has made it an attractive stopover for cruise trips.

...eclectic blend of Greek and Turkish qualities.

imaret

Located in the historical district of Kavala in northern Greece, the stunning Imaret hotel is an unexpected oasis of tranquillity, period architecture, lavish interiors, peaceful arcades and lush gardens.

The architectural monument is a timeless masterpiece of late Ottoman architecture, one of the few remaining in Europe. It was commissioned in 1817 by Mohamed Ali Pasha of Egypt, as a gift to the city of Kavala, his birthplace. Delicate domed roofs, arched ceilings and open-air portals create a complex union of interior and exterior spaces. Through the careful preservation efforts of a team of dedicated archaeologists and architects, this magnificent historic jewel was restored to its former glory.

Imaret offers 26 lavish rooms and suites—four deluxe guestrooms for individual accommodation; 11 deluxe guestrooms for double occupancy; and 11 luxurious suites. Rooms are reminiscent of Arabian boudoirs, with ornate oriental carpets and lush fabrics, while others have domed ceilings adorned with antique chandeliers, as Byzantine Chapels. Period furniture has been selectively collected, restored to its full glory and tastefully arranged in this monumental masterpiece.

Guest quarters are seasonally draped with lush velvets and silks for cooler months, and handpicked French and Egyptian linens during balmy weather. Bathrooms provide crisply pressed brocade cottons amidst mosaic tiles, sunken baths and copper-encrusted

THIS PAGE (FROM LEFT): The tranquil gardens lull one into relaxation with gentle sounds of water; suites are adorned with period furniture and lush fabrics.

OPPOSITE (FROM LEFT): The Imaret's central location allows one to enjoy vistas over Kavala port; pamper yourself as the Sultans did, at the Imaret Spa.

rooms
26 lavish rooms and suites

food
Imaret Restaurant: seasonal menus • organic fruit and vegetable garden • tea room: vintage porcelain, crystal and silver service

drink
Imaret Bar: wine, malts and cognac menu • Gardens of Mohamed Ali Pasha

features
Imaret Spa: hammam, cistern indoor spa pool, outdoor pool • helicopter service • wireless Internet • business and secretarial services • conference and meeting rooms

nearby
Museum of Mohamed Ali Pasha • Estate Biblia Chora winery • Thassos Island • ancient city of Amphipolis • Nestos' aquatic biotope • Paggeon Monasteries • Byzantine castles of Thrace • Mount Athos • Philippi site

contact
30–32 Theodore Poulidou Street, 65110 Kavala • telephone: +30.2510.620 151 • facsimile: +30.2510.620 156 • email: info@imaret.gr • website: www.imaret.com

sinks. In-room toiletries include a selection of Bulgari White complemented by Molton Brown for sensual indulgence.

All rooms and suites encompass the vast inner courtyard, whose gardens and marbled arcades reflect the original grandeur of Imaret's 19th-century Islamic gardens. The diverse selection of botanicals and hushed whisper of fountains and pools create a backdrop of supreme relaxation.

The restaurant, situated beneath a glass façade, is a blend of Mediterranean scenery, fine wine and haute cuisine. The seasonal menu offers local and European specialities coupled with world-class regional wines. Fruits, vegetables and aromatic herbs are all cultivated from Imaret's own organic garden. Delicate crystal stemware, vintage porcelain and fine silver facilitate a superb dining experience. After dinner, retire to the Gardens of Mohamed Ali Pasha, which offer stunning views of the old port. The fine champagnes, single malts and cognacs are sure to satisfy even the most disciplined palette.

During warmer months, private dining is available in the gardens and on the terraces. Breakfast, afternoon coffee and high tea are served, with an extensive selection of teas from around the world, all presented on vintage Haviland porcelain tea service.

Women of the east have long been famed for their skin of silk. The Imaret Spa continues this tradition through the spa's signature hammam and massage treatments. Essential oils, herbs, restorative antioxidants, AHA fruit scrubs, aromatherapy, perfumed oil rubs and specialised massages allow guests to relax, rebalance and renew both body and soul.

alpha estate

Named after the first letter of the Greek alphabet and the first letter of the Amyndeon area where it is located, as well as the word used to describe anything of top quality in spoken Greek, Alpha Estate is the brainchild of oenologist and winemaker, Angelos Iatridis. He describes the estate as a renaissance for Greek wine, where technology meets finesse.

After formal education at the University of Bordeaux and the Universite du Vin de Suze la Rousse in France, Iatridis returned to Greece. He advised various top Greek vineyards and wineries as a consulting oenologist for several years. With his experience and insight, Iatridis is considered a key figure in the contemporary Greek wine industry.

In 1997, Iatridis began buying land in the Amyndeon plateau area of western Macedonia, the coldest winemaking region of Greece. Before the end of the decade, Makis Mavridis, partner and expert 3rd generation vinegrower, had planted over 65 hectares (161 acres) of grapes in Amyndeon and kicked off the development of a sophisticated and state-of-the-art vineyard.

Alpha Estate's mission is to make wines that display the region's unique geography. The local microclimate offers moderate temperatures and heavy rain in the winter— often light snow—resulting in conditions ideal for grape ripening. The nearby Petron and Vegoritida lakes contribute to the semi-

THIS PAGE (FROM LEFT): Angelos Iatradis and Makis Mavridis are the people behind this world-renowned vineyard; the estate cultivates 12 different grape varieties.

OPPOSITE (FROM LEFT): The estate often experiences snow in winter, creating prime grape-ripening conditions; Alpha Estate's wines enjoy international acclaim.

continental climate, which favours the growth of foreign and domestic varieties of both white and red grapes.

The estate uses cutting-edge vinicultural practices and technology, using computers to monitor variables such as temperature and moisture levels, and it consistently invests in new research with the aim of improving the quality of its wines. Some of the grape varieties grown on the estate include Sauvignon Blanc, Malagouzia, Syrah, Merlot, Mavrodaphne, Tannat, Pinot Noir, Barbera, Montepulciano and Xinomavro, among others.

Alpha Estate's wines have received accolades from a number of sources. Serena Sutcliffe, Master of Wine and Head of Sotheby's International Wine says, 'Alpha Estate Red 2004 is a most exciting and unusual auction find.' Much praise has also come from the international wine magazine *Decanter*—in the 2008 Decanter World Wine Awards, Alpha Estate Red 2005 received a Regional Trophy for best Greek Red Wine, and four other labels took gold and silver. It comes as no surprise that one can find Alpha Estate's wines at some of the most outstanding restaurants of the world, such as Chanterelle and South Gate in Manhattan.

Visitors are welcome to arrange private tours of the estate. It makes an excellent stop on the scenic drive from Thessaloniki to the Prespa Lakes or Pindos National Park.

products
red and white wines from domestic and foreign grape varieties

recommendations
Alpha Estate Red: Syrah, Merlot and Xinomavro • Alpha Estate White: Sauvignon Blanc • Alpha Xinomavro • Alpha Syrah • Alpha Pinot Noir • Alpha Chardonnay • Alpha One: a premium selection of the best 17 barrels produced • Omega dessert wine: Gewürztraminer and Malagouzia

features
private tours of the estate vineyards and winery • wine tastings • forthcoming hotel and wine spa • renewable energy production

nearby
Petron and Vogorítas lakes • Kaimaktsalan and Vigla ski centres • Village of Nimfaio • Arktouros bear and wolf resorts

contact
2nd Km Amyndeon–Agios Panteleimonas 53200 Amyndeon, Florina • telephone: +30.23860.20 111 • facsimile: +30.23860.20 132 • email: info@alpha-estate.com • website: www.alpha-estate.com

domaine gerovassiliou

Just outside the village of Epanomi in northern Greece lies Domaine Gerovassiliou. This 53-hectare (131-acre), single-vineyard estate needs little introduction, and the same is true of its owner. Evangelos Gerovassiliou has been described as a 'celebrated winemaker' by Jancis Robinson, one of the world's leading authorities on wine. The vintages here are considered some of the best in the world, and Evangelos has been recognised for changing the perception of Greek wine internationally as well as for reviving Malagousia—an ancient, almost extinct grape variety.

The winery comprises four sections, the earliest dating back to the early 1980s. The private estate includes the vineyard and manor house; a contemporary tasting room; a wine museum purportedly housing one of the first wine bottles ever produced and a collection of over 2,000 corkscrews pre-dating the 18th century; and an high-tech production facility.

Hailed as a visionary of Greek wine, Evangelos holds impeccable winemaking credentials. A graduate of Oenology and Viticulture from Bordeaux University in France, he also trained under the legendary professor of oenology, Emile Peynaud. In 1976, Evangelos became the first Greek winemaker to engage in systematic cultivation of French grape varieties as a consulting oenologist at Domaine Porto Carras, one of Greece's most ambitious wine ventures. His vineyard's

THIS PAGE (FROM LEFT): Evangelos Gerovassiliou is the driving force behind the wine estate; the museum showcases rare wine artefacts, with a collection that spans centuries.

OPPOSITE (FROM LEFT): The vineyards of Domaine Gerovassiliou have expanded to over five times the estate's original size; the estate also arranges tours and private wine tastings.

history dates back to 1981, when Evangelos began planting a variety of both Greek and foreign grape varieties on a family owned 'ktima'—the Greek word for estate. Now near-synonymous with an international benchmark of gold-standard wines, Domaine Gerovassiliou has been described as the 'Greatest Greek Wine Producer from 2004 through 2008' by authors and experts Tom Stevenson and Nico Manessis.

One could even say that the ancient gods of Mount Olympus have smiled favourably upon Evangelos Gerovassiliou over the years. All of the estate's wines have received numerous awards and honours in prestigious international wine competitions, due to their consistent high quality.

All of the winery's grapes are single-estate cultivated. Greek varieties include Malagousia, Assyrtiko, Limnio, Mavrtotragano and Mavroudi, and French counterparts Chardonnay, Syrah, Viognier, Grenache Rouge, Sauvignon Blanc and Merlot. All wines are classified as 'Regional Wines of Epanomi' and Domaine Gerovassiliou was hailed as one of the 'Top 100 Wineries of the World in 2006' by *Wine & Spirits* magazine. Evangelos Gerovassiliou has also been named one of the best six winemakers worldwide in the Wine Awards 2007 by German magazine, *Wein Gourmet*. A quarter of the estate's production commands an international audience, with exports reaching Japan, North and South America, Europe and the UK.

products
red and white wines from Greek and French grape varieties

recommendations
Domaine Gerovassiliou White-Malagousia • Domaine Gerovassiliou Chardonnay • Domaine Gerovassiliou Red • Domaine Gerovassiliou Syrah • Domaine Gerovassiliou Avaton

features
guided tours • private wine tastings • tasting room • wine museum

nearby
Epanomi town • Cape Epanomi lighthouse • Mount Olympus • churches • ancient tombs

contact
Epanomi, 57500 Thessaloniki •
telephone: +30.23920.44 567 •
facsimile: +30.23920.44 560 •
email: ktima@gerovassiliou.gr •
website: www.gerovassiliou.gr

kir-yianni

The Kir-Yianni Estate was founded in 1997 by Yiannis Boutaris, one of the leading figures in the Greek wine industry. Known locally as the 'pope of wine', Yiannis has dedicated his life to promoting Greek vintages both at home and abroad. Kir-Yianni Estate actually comprises two estates in the wine regions of Naoussa and Amyndeon, on both sides of Mount Vermio in northwestern Greece. The winery focuses on the production of high-quality wines using high-tech viticulture practices which combine respect for the environment with authenticity and finesse. It was Yiannis Boutaris' intention to keep the winery in the family by educating his sons in the ways of business and wine. Today, the Kir-Yianni Estate is lead by eldest son and INSEAD graduate Stellios Boutaris,

who continues his father's original vision, tradition and philosophy. Mihalis Boutaris, the younger of the two, is a graduate of Harvard and the renowned viticulture school at the University of California, Davis, and now directs the vineyard's research and development.

The estate in Naoussa—one of Greece's leading AOC regions—is set at Yianakohori, the highest point of the viticultural region. The creation of the 50-hectare (124 acre) vineyard culminated in the revival of the prized Naoussa appellation and paved the way for a whole new generation of winemakers. The region's unique microclimate favours the cultivation of Xinomavro, the indigenous Greek grape, as well as other foreign varieties suitable for long ageing. It is

THIS PAGE (FROM LEFT): *Yiannis Boutaris' goal was to make Kir-Yianni a family vineyard; visitors should not miss the opportunity to tour the vineyards and winery.*
OPPOSITE (FROM LEFT): *The estate's vineyards are all cultivated using organic practices; Kir-Yianni's wines are sought after in all parts of the world.*

products
red and white wines from domestic and foreign grape varieties

recommendations
Kir-Yianni Estate 'Yianakohori' : dry red, Vin-de-Pays Imathia •
Ramnista: dry red, AOC Naoussa •
Dyo Elies: dry red, Vin-de-Pays Imathia •
Tesseris Limnes: dry white, Vin-de-Pays Florina •
Samaropetra: dry white, Vin-de-Pays Florina •
Petra: dry white, Vin-de-Pays Florina •
Akakies: dry rosé, AOC Amyndeon •
Paranga: dry red, Vin-de-Pays Macedonia

features
private tours of the estate and vineyards •
private wine tastings • tasting room •
exhibition facility

nearby
Mount Vermio • Petron and Vegoritis Lakes •
Kaimaktsalan and Vigla ski centres • Village of
Nimfaio • Arktouros bear and wolf preserves

contact
Yianakohori, 59200 Naoussa •
telephone: +30.23320.51 100 •
facsimile: +30.23320.51 140 •
email: info@kiryianni.gr •
website: www.kiryianni.gr

here that the estate's flagship wine, Yianakohori, is produced. Other notable wines are Ramnista, made purely from Xinomavro grapes, and the super-blend, Dyo Elies. At the heart of the family estate is the *koula* or *konaki*, a traditional watchtower which has become the emblem of the winery.

Covering 165 hectares (408 acres), the Amyndeon estate and winery is located in the winemaking village of Ayios Panteleimon at the shores of Lake Vegoritis, bordered by the Kaimaktsalan and Vitsi mountains. Once neglected, the Amyndeon region is now recognised as one of the most promising AOC zones in Greece, thanks to the efforts of Yiannis Boutaris. The terroir is characterised by a unique

microclimate, due to its high altitude (700 m, or 2,297 ft) and the four neighbouring lakes. At the estate, international white varieties such as Sauvignon Blanc, Chardonnay, Gewurztraminer and Viognier are cultivated alongside indigenous varieties such as Roditis, Assyrtiko, Malagousia and Malvasia Aromatica. The estate produces four distinct wines: Tesseris Limnes, a unique blend of Chardonnay and Gewurtraminer, Samaropetra, made from Sauvignon Blanc and Roditis, Petra from pure Roditis, and Akakies, a refreshing rosé wine.

Stellios Boutaris has invested heavily in the vineyards since assuming his role. He believes that 'good wines are made in the winery, but great wines are made in the vineyard.'

ktima biblia chora

On the slopes of Mount Pangeon in northern Greece, oenologists Vassilis Tsaktsarlis and Evangelos Gerovassiliou have united to create Ktima Biblia Chora. One of Greece's most exciting new boutique wineries, Ktima Biblia Chora needs little introduction. The name comes from the grapes brought by the ancient Phoenicians from the eastern shores of the Mediterranean. The variety was called 'Biblos' and the region became known as Biblia Chora.

The estate consists of a Bordeaux-styled château; a contemporary tasting room in the ktima's cellar, which has hundreds of French oak barrels installed in lit alcoves; a cutting-edge production facility; and 35 hectares (86 acres) of vineyards. Elevation and weather unite to create a grape-growing season nearly two weeks longer than other parts of the Greek peninsula. In summer, the vineyards receive a cooling downdraft from the peaks above them; in winter, the nearby Aegean Sea significantly tempers the climate. The partners aimed to concentrate the vineyards on the southern slopes, which would yield the maximum amount of fruit at the acidity levels they were anticipating.

THIS PAGE (FROM LEFT): Estate Biblia Chora is a dynamic synergy by renowned oenologists Vassilis Tsaktsarlis and Evangelos Gerovassiliou; wines are stored in oak casks until their desired age.

OPPOSITE (FROM LEFT): The main winery is designed in the style of a Bordeaux château; private tastings and tours are available by appointment.

products
red and white wines from domestic and foreign grape varieties

recommendations
Biblia Chora White: Assyrtiko and Sauvignon Blanc · Biblia Chora Rosé: Syrah · Biblia Chora Red: Merlot and Cabernet Sauvignon · Biblia Chora Merlot · Biblia Chora Chardonnay · Ovilos White: Assyrtiko and Semillon · Ovilos Red: Cabernet Sauvignon · Areti White: Assyrtiko · Areti Red: Agiorgitiko

features
guided tours of the estate and vineyards by appointment · private tastings

nearby
Mount Pangeon · Aegean Sea · Imaret Hotel

contact
Kokkinochori, 64008 Kavala ·
telephone: +30.25920.44 974 ·
facsimile: +30.25920.44 975 ·
email: ktima@bibliachora.gr ·
website: www.bibliachora.gr

Despite the 16-year age difference, the partners' similar backgrounds helped create a dynamic synergy. Tsaktsarlis and Gerovassiliou were both born in Epanomi, educated at the University of Thessaloniki and later the University of Bordeaux in France. They first met in 1988; Gerovassiliou was Chief Oenologist at Domaine Porto Carras and Tsaktsarlis was at the beginning of his winemaking career. The first vines of their collective estate were planted in 1998 and the subsequent fruits of their labour were presented in 2001.

Wine authority Jancis Robinson praises Biblia Chora White 2006—'what a delicious blend of Sauvignon and Assyrtiko... with the minerals and lemon of Assyrtiko with real raciness and fresh pungency of the Sauvignon Blanc, yet vinified with such gentle hand that the impression is one of a particularly delicate wine.' The unique Biblia Chora Rosé—100 percent Syrah—bears a vivid pomegranate colour and is in a class all its own. The ktima's handcrafted wines perform exceptionally well at international competitions. The single-estate wines have received numerous distinctions and trophies over the years from competitions such as the Decanter—International Trophy for Biblia Chora White 2004 and Ovilos White 2005—as well as Germany's Mundus VINI, where Ovilos White 2003 was hailed as the 'Best Dry White Wine in Europe'.

Greek varieties cultivated include Assyrtiko and Agiorgitiko, while foreign varieties include Sauvignon Blanc, Chardonnay, Semillon, Syrah, Merlot and Cabernet Sauvignon. The ktima is a certified organic producer and organic vineyard.

islandgreece

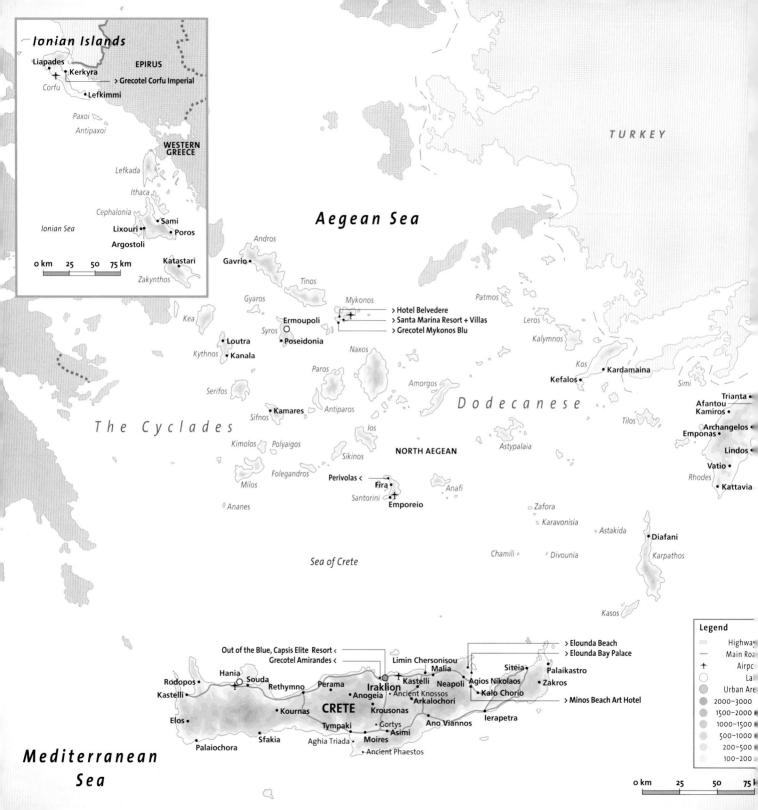

island greece

They may represent but a fraction of the total land area, but the far-flung Greek isles—with their brightly coloured fishing boats, turquoise coves and striking cubist architecture—have come to represent for many all that is quintessentially Greek. And there are certainly plenty to go around. A determined island-hopper could conceivably set foot on a different Greek island every day for 16 years and still not see them all. There are more than 6,000 islands in total, parcelled out among the Aegean, the Ionian and the Sea of Crete. Some of them—such as Mykonos and Santorini—are synonymous with the jet-set crowd who first made Greece a global holiday spot in the 1960s. Others are virtually unknown to outsiders, such as the sparsely inhabited Sporades where much of the film version of *Mamma Mia!* was shot.

While sunseeking is undoubtedly a main attraction, the islands have plenty of other guilty pleasures as well. The seafood is divine, especially when consumed alongside copious amounts of *ouzo* and wine at any of the waterfront tavernas. The nightlife on party-mad Mykonos is also world-renowned. Almost non-existent 30 years ago, shopping has improved by leaps and bounds, especially in the busier ports. There's even a fair bit of history for visitors looking to while the day away amid age-old ruins instead of on the beach. And while many choose to tour the Greek isles aboard a cruise ship or a chartered yacht, a comprehensive ferry network between the islands and from Athens makes for easy commuting.

crete

The elongated island of Crete is almost like a small country unto itself. One soon realises that while Cretans are thoroughly Greek they are also vastly different, the result of both the island's isolation from the mainland—of all the Greek isles, Crete is the farthest south—and its long history of foreign occupation. In more recent times, Crete has been known for providing the gorgeous seaside backdrop against which films such as Greek director Yannis Smaragdis' *El Greco* have been shot.

Iraklion is the island's *de facto* political and commercial capital, and the gateway through which most visitors arrive. Hania offers easy access to the western portion of the island, while Akrotiri's lush nature and rocky coast line is accompanied by stunning views. Central Iraklion is flanked by massive Venetian walls and gates, with the harbour mouth protected by the 16th-century Koules fort. Rather than follow a traditional grid pattern, Ikralion is laid out in a circular manner with major streets converging at the busy Plateia Venizelou (Freedom Square) in the middle. On the outskirts of Iraklion is the island's most impressive archaeological site—the ruins of ancient Knossos. From 2000–1250 BC, Knossos served as the religious and ruling nexus for the Minoan civilisation. Much of the civilisation remains a mystery; however, the period's achievements greatly influenced the subsequent development of classical Greece.

THIS PAGE: *Simi, a small island in the Dodecanese chain is well-known as both a yacht haven and the venue for its summer-long arts festival.*

PAGE 116: *The whitewashed Oia village clings to the volcanic cliffs along the edge of Santorini's volcanic caldera.*

THIS PAGE: *The windmills of Mykonos stand alongside the Parthenon as one of Greece's most recognisable landmarks.*

OPPOSITE (FROM TOP): *From* Zorba the Greek *to* Mamma Mia!, *dancing has long defined the Greek island experience; a plethora of al fresco cafés sprawl along the waterfront of the Little Venice district of Chora on Mykonos.*

Crete's most popular beach strip is along the Mirambelo Gulf, where a mixed bag of bargain and upscale resorts cater to the international sun, sand and sea crowd. Agios Nikolaos, another former Venetian outpost, centres around a small saltwater inlet called Lake Voulismeni and an old town flush with nightlife and sidewalk cafés. Most of the high-end hotels and villas are situated along Elounda Beach, with its offerings of gourmet dining establishments, sophisticated clubs and posh resorts. Nearby, the abandoned remains of a fort and leper colony on Spinalonga island exude an aura of mystery that continually attracts tourist hordes.

Much of Crete's south coast remains wild and untamed, in particular a spectacular natural chasm called the Samaria Gorge. The national park features rich island flora and endangered wildlife, as well as a popular 16-km (10-mile) hiking trail along the rugged White Mountains, *Lefka Ori*—with peaks as high as 2000 metres (1,243 feet).

the cyclades

The Cyclades archipelago is undoubtedly a classic representation of all the Aegean has to offer: a timeless landscape of whitewashed villages on desert-like islands, sapphire sea set against an equally deep-blue sky, and folk tunes drifting from waterfront tavernas. The name Cyclades ('to circle') derives from the fact that the islands surrounded the ancient Greek shrine on Delos. Coincidentally, the islands also lie at the geographic centre of the Aegean. There are more than 200 islands in total, but only two dozen support any sort of commerce and are home to handfuls of residents.

Once the bastion of quiet fishing villages, the Cyclades have evolved over the past 30 years into one of Europe's most important holiday destinations. While tourism is the major economic mover and shaker, the islands also make a living from agriculture and wine production. Although occupied as early as 5,000 BC, the arid, rocky and often volcanic landscape on these islands hindered the development of powerful city-states, as in the case of Crete and the mainland.

cosmopolitan mykonos

Mykonos may not be the largest or the most populated of the Cyclades, but it is certainly the most well-known, attracting a steady stream of cosmopolitan travellers. Lifestyles of the rich and famous play out at the island's many posh resorts and restaurants, with Mykonos boasting the best dining, shopping and clubbing scenes among all the Aegean islands, if not the entire Mediterranean. Alternative lifestyles—hippies, artists, nudists and gays—also flourish on an island known for its 'anything goes' attitude.

Once upon a time, fishing and farming were the island's main avenues of revenue. These days though, tourism—along with the infrastructure and professions that support it—is by far the largest employer. Such is the case for many of the more populous Greek isles, but dependence on visitors is especially acute on Mykonos, a rocky and largely barren island that would not be able to support its 9,300 inhabitants without pandering to the countless hip travellers and all that they have come to expect.

Despite its heavy reliance on tourism, Mykonos still manages to retain much of its picturesque charm. Chora, the island's photogenic capital and port, depicts this contradiction best. Wrapped around a U-shaped bay, the town's cobblestone lanes are flanked by rustic townhouses with bright blue window shutters. Mykonos may be home to over 250 churches, but the 15th-century Panagia Paraportiani church complex stands out easily with its eclectic mix of Byzantium and local architectural elements, culminating in a whitewashed structure that seems to melt beneath the Aegean sun.

Little Venice district encapsulates the hip, edgy side of Mykonos with its array of stylish bars and restaurants suspended over the water. Nearby, the iconic windmills of Kato Myli cut a dramatic figure against the evening sky, while farther south, the über-trendy Ornos and Psarou beaches prepare for yet another night of hedonistic revelry.

Shops around Chora boast a wide variety of fashion from Greek *haute couture* to bohemian summer frocks. While Chora has its fair share of quaint tavernas serving superb Greek cuisine, it also offers world-class cuisines and talents from around the globe. At Matsuhisa Mykonos, celebrity chef Nobu Matsuhisa's distinctive culinary style adds yet another touch of sophistication to this already fashionable locale. Late-night party-goers have no shortage of places to hang out, and Mykonos' pulsating club scene sees hardcore clubbers thronging the hectic line-up of parties, posh soirées and international DJ gigs throughout the summer.

From Chora harbour, ferries ply back and forth to Delos, the legendary birthplace of Apollo and a place of religious pilgrimage for more than a thousand years. The tiny island's considerable ruins include temples, villas with rich mosaics and the renowned Terrace of the Lions.

spectacular santorini

Another Cycladic island that stands out for its raw beauty is Santorini (Thera), formed by a massive volcanic eruption circa 1600 BC and possibly where the legend of the lost city of Atlantis originated from. The island wraps around three sides of the flooded caldera, with the main town and numerous villages perched hundreds of metres above the water. From a distance, the ancient whitewashed skyline resembles a glacier or snowpack along the caldera's upper edge.

Much like Mykonos, traditional island life on Santorini has been largely superseded by the advent of tourism. A delightful exception is viniculture, an island staple since at least the Bronze Age. Given its hot, dry climate and volcanic soil, perhaps it comes as no surprise that Santorini is especially adept at cultivating the Assyrtiko, Athiri and Aidani grape varieties used to produce fine white wines for which Santorini AOC is justly famous. Due to the intense sun, cool evenings and relentless winds, the vines are kept low to the ground and shaped into circular basket-shaped forms called *ampelies* to protect the grapes from the elements. And because the island was one of the few places in Europe spared by the devastating phylloxera wine plague in the mid 19th century, many of the wines are of original root stock stretching back more than 200 years old.

There are numerous ways one could spend the day in Santorini. One could plan a whole afternoon around Greek archaeology with visits to the Museum of Ancient Thera with its mosaic masterpieces and the Minoan ruins of Akrotiri. Another day could be spent trekking the precipitous footpath between the main towns of Oia and Fira—camera in hand, of course,

THIS PAGE: Many high-end resorts offer the option of swimming in a pool or the sea, complete with mesmerising vistas of Santorini.

OPPOSITE: Whitewashed walls and blue domes mark Santorini as one of the most picturesque of the Aegean isles.

because around every corner is another stunning vista, especially in the village of Imerovigli with its blue-domed churches. Likewise, a shopping expedition in Oia or Fira will require a full day with plenty of reproductions of ancient artwork and handcrafted contemporary or Minoan jewellery to choose from.

Travellers who prefer to experience indigenous Greece should pay a visit to the other Cycladic Islands. Far more laidback in character, the smaller islands are home to the local fishermen and farmers whose friendly demeanour is apparent regardless of their limited English.

With its busy harbour, Paros is the ferry hub of the archipelago. Neighbouring Naxos is the largest of the Cyclades. Known for its wealth of Byzantine churches, it is also a great place for hiking in the backcountry and sunbathing on the virtually empty beaches. Way over in the west, the island of Milos is renowned for its stark volcanic landscapes and ancient masterpieces. The armless Aphrodite of Milos—or as many know her, the Venus de Milo—is one such example, and can still be viewed at the Lourve in Paris today.

the dodecanese

True to its name, the Dodecanese ('Twelve Islands') comprises a dozen major islands in the far eastern Aegean along the Turkish coast. Rhodes is the largest, with a land area greater than all of the other islands combined. Famed for the now-demolished Colossus of Rhodes—a gargantuan statue that stood at the harbour entrance and one of the Seven Wonders of the Ancient World—Rhodes is much more multicultural in character compared to the other Greek isles. The Romans, Byzantines, Crusaders, Ottomans and Italians all left their mark on the island, as can be seen from the eclectic architecture of mosques, domed churches and medieval battlements.

Life still centres around Rhodes' Old Town, enclosed by stout walls and entered via ancient gateways. In the midst of bustling shops and cafés sits the impressive 14th-century Palace of the Grand Master. Originally built by the Knights of Rhodes, the palace was later used by the king of Italy and Benito Mussolini as a summer home. In 1522, the Ottomans' victory over the Christian stronghold saw the establishment of the Mosque of Suleiman on Socratous Street, yet another indication of the island's political importance to the various superpowers during the Middle Ages.

Given the island's close proximity to Turkey, Old Town offers a multitude of Greek and Middle Eastern treasures to discover and bring home. Exotic rugs, handmade vases and reproduction icons can be found in many local boutiques, alongside gold, silver and platinum jewellery. Despite being a tourist magnet, a healthy portion of Rhodes' nightspot clientele remains Greek, evident from the various local music bars and clubs in Old Town. Visitors will also come across live music bars catering to foreigners, although 'clubbing staples' such as techno trance gigs will have to be found outside Old Town. Noise pollution has been elevated to such a critical level that locals have begun campaigning for the ousting of loud nightspots from within the town walls.

Patmos stands out as the place where St John the Theologian spent several years in exile composing the Book of Revelation. His memory lingers on in the medieval Monastery of St John the Theologian and the Cave of the Apocalypse (a UNESCO world heritage site); both places remain important destinations among Orthodox and Western Christian pilgrims. Another draw is the island's stunning beaches of Psili Ammos, Agriolivadi, Grikos and Cambos—all of which are much less crowded than those of the main islands.

THIS PAGE: Narrow alleyways that lead straight out to sea are a distinctive feature of the Dodecanese Islands.

OPPOSITE: A couple strolls around the Palace of the Grand Master, which was built as a symbol of Christian power in the 14th century.

Once reputed for its boat builders, the island of Simi is now internationally famous for its summer-long Simi Festival, a celebration of music, dance, performance and visual arts as well as ancient Greek ideals. Artists are not paid to perform: it is purely gratis. Likewise, the performances are complimentary for the public and seating is on a first-come, first-served basis. Yet summer after summer, the festival attracts the brightest of Greek musicians, dancers and actors.

the ionian islands: corfu

Around the western side of Greece lie the Ionian islands. The archipelago stands out from other Greek isles because of its unique blend of Hellenic, Venetian and British colonial influences.

The biggest of the Ionian chain is Cephalonia, known for its pristine natural beauty and endangered loggerhead turtles, the *Karreta Karreta*. Although the island's location near a tectonic fault line has subjected it to various earthquakes over the years, Cephalonia's luxuriant verdure and beaches continually attract nature lovers, and it was here where the film *Captain Corelli's Mandolin* was shot. Nearby is Ithaca, the island kingdom of Homer's legendary Odysseus. The municipality is also known to possess one of the largest natural harbours in the world.

Corfu is the second-largest and most populous island, a diverse spot with a complex past, lush vegetation—the island receives the most rainfall in Greece—and a long history as a regal getaway. From 1386 to 1797, Corfu was ruled by Venetian nobility. In the late 19th century, the island was part of the far-flung British Empire and became a holiday haunt for the likes of Queen Victoria and the Empress 'Sisi' of Austria-Hungary. Despite much destruction during WWII, the old town of Corfu is renowned for its Venetian architecture, best depicted in structures such as the Old Venetian Fortress, the Liston arcades on the Esplanade, the 17th-century City Hall and the Mon Repos Palace, birthplace of Prince Philip, Duke of Edinburgh—also Philippos of Greece and Denmark—royal consort to Queen Elizabeth II of England .

Similar to Provence and Tuscany, Corfu has become a haven for those seeking mild winters and Mediterranean landscapes, while recent upheavals in Eastern Europe have also seen migrants gravitating to this sunny locale. Agriculture is very much a part of Corfu's scenic landscape: olives, pomegranates, figs, grapes, almonds, prickly pears and bananas are commonly cultivated..

Located at the bottom of the Adriatic, Corfu is a sailing paradise with numerous isles, coves and inlets to explore. Scuba diving is also popular, with the underwater landscape filled with intriguing rock formations and wrecks. Back on land, Corfu's craggy terrain is ideal for mountain biking and trekking. Taking visitors high above sea level through verdant woodland and forgotten pathways, the Corfu Trail offers a scenic introduction to the island's interior with its well-maintained villages, archaeological sites, Byzantium ruins and bucolic vistas of wildflowers and age-old cypress trees.

THIS PAGE: A great many of the cobblestone lanes and back streets of Corfu seem little changed by 21st-century life.

OPPOSITE: Columns topped by bronze deer mark what is believed to be the place where the Colossus of Rhodes once straddled the entrance of the island's main harbour.

a haven for those seeking mild winters and Mediterranean landscapes...

hotel belvedere

The comforts offered by Belvedere Hotel guarantee a good night's rest, but waking up is even better. The mesmerising morning sun reflects off the sandy white beaches of Mykonos, and the luxurious suites invite one to lounge around and enjoy breakfast in bed.

Facing the Aegean Sea, Belvedere Hotel has 35 rooms and eight suites in six categories, each catering to the needs and expectations of different guests. Inspired by the waters of the sapphire sea and the immaculate white houses on the island, every room has pristine plaster walls with a matching ceiling made from Mykonian wood, crystal ice marble flooring and subtle lighting that adds to the cosy ambience. Ergonomic designer furniture offers understated luxury and functionality that enhances the living experience.

All rooms are sound-proofed to ensure a peaceful stay, while air-conditioning and floor heating ensure guests remain comfortable regardless of the season. Rooms are fitted with state-of-the-art entertainment systems. Guests can 'spin' their own music with the iPod docking stations, which are connected to stereo surround-sound systems with integrated sub woofers—perfect for the aspiring DJ. They can also tune into their favourite channel, watch DVDs on the flat-screen TV or catch up with their friends and families with wireless Internet connection.

Dining at the Belvedere Hotel can be an enlightening experience. The eponymous Matsuhisa Mykonos is operated by renowned chef Nobu Matsuhisa, who is acclaimed for his unique fusion of Japanese ingredients with

THIS PAGE (FROM LEFT): *The Belvedere Suite has a terrace from which one can admire the bay; the hotel's décor matches the pure white houses of Mykonos.*

OPPOSITE (FROM LEFT): *Matsuhisa Mykonos is renowned for its unique menu of Japanese and Peruvian fusion cuisine; have a drink mixed by Dale de Groff at the Belvedere Bar.*

rooms
35 rooms • 8 suites

food
Matsuhisa Mykonos: Japanese fusion •
Belvedere Club: Greek

drink
Belvedere Bar

features
Kiehls • wireless high-speed Internet access •
outdoor pool • 24-hour gym • jacuzzi •
steam room • music and movie library

nearby
beach • shopping arcade

contact
School of Fine Arts District, 84600 Mykonos •
telephone: +30.22890.25 122 •
facsimile: +30.22890.25 126 •
email: contact@belvederehotel.com •
website: www.belvederehotel.com

Peruvian influence. Some of his legendary dishes include tiradito, black cod with miso, and new-style sashimi. For Greek cuisine, diners can head to the Belvedere Club, with dishes created by celebrated Greek Australian chef George Callombaris. Kick back and relax after dinner with a cocktail mixed by famous mixologist Dale de Groff at the Belvedere Bar, or attend a wine-tasting session at the Matsuhisa wine cellar. With a staggering 5,000 bottles in its collection, the cellar has been consistently honoured with the 'Award of Excellence' from *Wine Spectator* since 2003.

Besides soaking up the sun on the beach or lounging at the pool bar, guests can also work their bodies out in the fully equipped fitness centre that remains open 24 hours. It has a stretching area, cardiovascular area and specialised equipment to cater to the needs of every guest. Otherwise, guests can choose to pamper themselves with massage therapies enhanced by fine aromatherapy essential oils and signature blends.

Guests can have their fix of retail therapy at the Belvedere shopping arcade. One can find all the casual clothing and beach wear needed for a day by the sea at the Belvedere Shop, along with unique accessories and cosmetics from various Greek and international designers. The hotel has also collaborated with New York-based cosmetics company Kiehls to bring guests an exclusive range of high-quality holistic beauty products and amenities.

Listed on *Lonely Planet*'s Bluelist of 'beaches to die for', there is no better place to be seen 'dead' on Mykonos than in Belvedere Hotel.

mykonos blu

One of the hippest destinations of the Cyclades islands, Mykonos is popular with both overseas visitors and fashionable Athenians who fly or sail to the islands for short getaways. Located on a bluff with panoramic views of Psarou beach, Mykonos Blu offers the perfect blend of privacy and easy access to the hip nightlife, culture and shopping that keeps visitors coming back.

Taking a cue from Cycladic architecture, this Grecotel Exclusive Resort resembles a traditional whitewashed village set against a backdrop of the Aegean sea. Villas, suites and bungalows nestle in a natural amphitheatre. The unique saltwater infinity pool looks out over the hotel's beautiful private beach.

Accommodations feature rustic interiors with cobalt blue accents typical of the region, but include all of the modern conveniences that one expects of a top-notch resort. Some have a private pool or an al fresco jacuzzi, private gardens, or a terrace with a gym. The extravagant bathrooms flaunt polished stone bathtubs and phototherapy showers.

THIS PAGE: Mykonos Blu stands over the Aegean Sea, offering gorgeous views of the water.

OPPOSITE (FROM LEFT): The white-and-blue décor scheme brings to mind Cycladic architecture; handcrafted artworks and sculptures add rustic appeal to the hotel's public spaces.

Designed to take full advantage of the brilliant Aegean light, all villas are ultra-spacious and breezy. Suites have their own shaded terraces, private pools and canopy beds draped in lush fabrics, filtering the sun's rays through half-open shutters.

Spacious bungalow suites offer separate living and sleeping quarters that spill onto a private terrace with sweeping views. All are individually decorated to offer the utmost in relaxation and comfort. Villas occupy prime sea-front property on a low incline over the beach. No two are the same, yet each is spacious and furnished to soothe and inspire.

The Aegean Poets restaurant serves outstanding Mediterranean cuisine, delicious Greek and seafood specialities. For more informal dining, L'Archipel brasserie offers local fare in a relaxed poolside atmosphere.

There is also the option of romantic dinners on the beach or in one's villa, private beach barbecues or in-room family-style meals.

Gorgeous views, sumptuous sofas and great drinks are the hallmarks of the Delos Lounge. Whether sipping *ouzo* or champagne as the sun sets or slipping in a quick drink before heading into town for the island's famous nightlife, this bar is a great place to chill out with friends.

Those in need of down time can head to the Elixir Fitness Spa & Gallery, reminiscent of a magical underwater grotto. Relax in the sauna before enjoying a massage, beauty treatment, or workout on the fitness equipment.

The resort is ideally situated for exploring the attractions of Mykonos Town. Hotel staff can arrange customised itineraries of the best restaurants, ateliers, art galleries and clubs.

rooms
111 bungalows, suites and villas

food
Aegean Poets: Mediterranean ·
L'Archipel: brasserie

drink
Delos Lounge

features
Elixir Fitness Spa & Gallery · saltwater infinity pool · beach · library · boutique · jewellery shop · jogging path

nearby
Mykonos Town · shopping · restaurants · nightlife · museums · chapels · art galleries

contact
Psarou, 84600 Mykonos ·
telephone: +30.22890.27 900 ·
facsimile: +30.22890.27 783 ·
e-mail: sales_mb@grecotel.gr ·
website: www.mykonosblu.com

santa marina resort + villas

THIS PAGE: Marine Club Restaurant
& Bar serves gourmet seafood
over views of the sparkling sea.

OPPOSITE (FROM LEFT): The Presidential
Diamond Villa is four storeys
tall with features such as a
private sauna, gym and pool;
take a cool dip under the stars.

On the island of Mykonos, a sprawling 8-hectare (20-acre) resort development of crisp white accommodations and villas descends the sides of a hill bordering the Aegean Sea. The buildings finally lead to a sandy private beach lapped by sparkling blue water. From virtually any spot on the Santa Marina Resort's grounds, the surrounding land lies open to the naked eye; the horizon is an unbroken stretch that signals one has arrived at a very special sort of paradise.

Although situated a scant 3 km (2 miles) from the lively nightlife scene and shops of Mykonos Town, the Santa Marina's sheltered coastal site grants it the tranquillity of a cosmopolitan lifestyle resort. It has been designed to provide everything necessary for a complete vacation without the need to venture out, although it is convenient to do so if one wishes. It pays strict attention to the privacy of guests—the compound is gated, visitors are regulated, and bodyguards are assigned upon request. The guarantee of privacy has attracted the patronage of international celebrities, who make up some of the resort's most appreciative regulars.

The Santa Marina's accommodations consist of both guest suites and private villas, so suitable rooms are available regardless of the size of the party. The 68 guestrooms, 20 suites and eight villas are certain to satisfy even the most picky traveller. Every room has its own balcony with panoramic views of the sea and nearby Ornos Bay. Their tasteful interiors reflect the philosophy that shaped the traditionally inspired buildings that house them. They work in tandem with Cycladic architectural forms to create an iconic Greek elegance. Modern conveniences such as flat-screen TVs with cable channels, minibars, DVD players and premium bathroom amenities are available for guests in all rooms.

rooms
68 rooms • 20 suites • 8 villas

food
Colonial Pool Restaurant & Bar: poolside breakfast buffets and all-day dining • Marine Club Restaurant & Bar: Mediterranean cuisine and fresh seafood • Beach Taverna & Bar: barbecues and Greek specialities

drink
pool bars and restaurants

features
Lotus Spa • private beach • 3 pools • watersports • tennis • gym • sauna and steam bath • helicopter, jet and limousine charters • speedboat charters • 24-hour room service

nearby
Mykonos Town: shopping, nightlife and restaurants • Delos • Paros • Naxos • Tinos • Siros

contact
Ornos Bay, 84600 Mykonos •
telephone: +30.22890.23 220 •
facsimile: +30.22890.23 412 •
email: info@santa-marina.gr •
website: www.santa-marina.gr

Guests for whom only the very best will do should consider booking one of the hillside villas. They have all the amenities enjoyed by the hotel rooms and, in addition, luxurious isolation. Of special note is the Presidential Diamond Villa. Its poolside view takes in all the surrounding islands and the nearby Mykonos Town. This villa has facilities to satisfy every whim, from working out at a private gym or relaxing in a sauna to lounging in one of the two living rooms complete with fireplaces and flat-screen televisions.

Those enjoying an intimate getaway may wish to dine privately, but the experience offered by the resort's restaurants should not be missed. Marine Club Restaurant & Bar presents gourmet seafood dishes prepared in Mediterranean style. They also serve fresh sushi, best enjoyed when paired with *sake* and views of the ocean. For guests who wish to get even closer to the water, there is the Beach Taverna & Bar. Diners can savour Greek cuisine, seafood and barbecued delicacies right on the resort's private beach.

Three pools are available for the use of all guests, as well as a full complement of leisure activities. Relax in the Lotus Spa, charter a speedboat or play tennis with the resident coach. With its impeccable service and exclusive surroundings, a stay at Santa Marina Resort & Villas makes one feel like a special sort of celebrity, too.

perivolas

Perched on the rim of the Santorini volcano, this hotel was developed over three decades by renovating 300-year-old wineries, cave homes and stables into 20 luxury suites. The local craftsmen who helped bring Perivolas back to life used volcanic stone as the basic material and finished everything off in striking white against Santorini's deep blue sky.

Suites in Perivolas are comfortable, light and airy, furnished in the simple yet elegant Cycladic style and dotted with interesting Aegean antiques. They are all individualised with small balconies and patios from which one can enjoy views of the ancient world's most celebrated caldera.

Offering what the owner Costis Psychas calls a 'mental detox', suites come without satellite televisions, DVD players and other electronic trappings. However, the suites are fully self-contained with kitchenettes, domed bathrooms with smooth concrete floors, and beds placed in individual alcoves.

Junior suites have open-plan layouts with the bedroom and sitting room integrated into a single, large space, while studios are smaller versions of the same. Superior suites flaunt a separate bedroom and living area. By far the most opulent are two individually designed Perivolas suites, which come complete with their own steam baths and private pools.

Set in a natural amphitheatre, the houses tumble down to a stone plaza where an old winery has been converted into Perivolas' restaurant and bar. The buffet breakfast offers fresh, homemade bread and pastries, complemented with preserves and Greek

THIS PAGE (FROM LEFT): The resort's infinity pool seems to hover above the Aegean Sea; modern touches complement the elegance of the caves.

OPPOSITE (FROM LEFT): The Perivolas Suites are minimalist but don't skimp on luxuries, such as the hydrotherapy massage pools; perched on Santorini's vaunted cliffs, Perivolas is a hideaway with its own Garden of Eden.

rooms
20 suites

food
restaurant: Mediterranean

drink
restaurant bar

features
wellness centre · fitness studio · library · infinity pool · jacuzzi · travel desk · Internet access

nearby
Santorini volcano · town with historical architecture, markets, cafés and restaurants · archaeological site

contact
Oia, 84702 Santorini ·
telephone: +30.22860.71 308 ·
facsimile: +30.22860.71 309 ·
email: info@perivolas.gr ·
website: www.perivolas.gr

yoghurt, as well as fresh fruits and juices. Breakfast in bed is an option for those who find it difficult to part from the comforts of their suite. The chef has crafted separate lunch and dinner menus which feature gourmet Mediterranean cuisine. Those who wish to enjoy an intimate meal may also arrange to dine in their own rooms.

Perhaps the most stunning aspect of Perivolas is the infinity pool, which seems to hover above the Aegean, colours matching so perfectly that the boundaries between manmade and nature are blurred. The organic shape of the pool and surroundings offer nooks that can be used for swimming, sunbathing or watching the sunset over Oia town. Complete the experience with a glass of wine from the resort's extensive cellar.

Although Perivolas does relish in its simplicity, daily newspapers are provided and there is Internet access, a small library and travel desk. It also boasts a fitness studio and wellness centre which offers massages, beauty and health treatments as well as a steam bath, sauna and open-air jacuzzi.

The friendly and helpful staff can also arrange guided tours, sailing, scuba diving, car and motorbike rentals, as well as chartered Lear jet service. They can advise on the best local walks and what not to miss in town.

Although Perivolas offers the utmost privacy, it is mere steps from the bustling town of Oia, with its array of cafés, boutiques and classy restaurants. Also nearby is the Bronze Age Akrotiri archaeological site and the Teleferic cable car, which can take one into the caldera.

amirandes

With elements of water, fire and earth, the stunning Amirandes resort is styled after the sprawling palaces of the Minoan kings and Venetian nobles that once ruled Crete. Situated on the north coast near Iraklion, this seafront resort is creatively arranged around reflecting pools and swimming areas that unite the hotel's sleek modern design.

Guests are sure to be impressed the moment they step into the lobby, with its huge picture windows and vista of the Aegean Sea. The view continues all the way through the resort's lush grounds, golden sands and cosmopolitan restaurants.

Accommodation runs an enticing gamut from luxury guestrooms in the main building to sophisticated private villas, all decorated in soft hues and cool fabrics. In keeping with the Creto-Venetian vibe, the villas are arranged in traditional Mediterranean village style, opening to natural stone terraces, palm trees and private pools on the beach.

No expense is spared in the furnishings and fittings, with many rooms offering private gyms, outdoor tropical rain showers and colour-therapy bathtubs. Standard in-room amenities include CD/DVD systems, flat-screen satellite televisions, wireless Internet access, individual climate control, minibars, and a fully stocked bathroom. Some even have a TV to ensure one's viewing experience remains uninterrupted while soaking.

For a truly unforgettable vacation, the Presidential Villa and Royal Residence offer the ultimate in luxury and privacy, apartment-sized beachfront properties equipped with the latest audiovisual entertainment units.

Amirandes boasts five exceptional and contrasting restaurants which take pride in sourcing locally for ingredients. Fresh organic fruit, vegetables, herbs and jams come directly from the Grecotel's nearby Agreco Farm.

rooms
212 rooms, suites, villas and residences

food
Amirandes: Mediterranean and international • Blue Monkey: Asian • Lago di Candia: international • Xasteria: Cretan • Petrino: Greek seafood • By the Pool: brasserie

drink
Labyrinth: Lounge bar

features
Elixir Spa • seawater pool • indoor pool • watersports • chapel • boutiques • golf course • tennis • multi-sports area • library • amphitheatre • meeting and function spaces

nearby
Iraklion • Knossos archaeological site • Crete golf club • Agreco Farm • CretAquarium • museums • water parks • horse riding

contact
P.O. Box 106, 71110 Iraklion, Crete • telephone: +30.28970.41 104 • facsimile: +30.28970.41 113 • email: sales_am@grecotel.gr • website: www.amirandes.com

Relaxed dining can be had poolside or in the Xasteria garden restaurant, while the avant-garde Blue Monkey serves modern twists on oriental delicacies cooked to order in a vivid 'Chinese red' setting. The freshest seafood—including Greek lobster and grouper—is served al fresco at Petrino. Old-world Mediterranean glamour is the draw of the 'floating' Amirandes signature restaurant, which features extensive buffets and show cooking, while the elegant Lago di Candia features an à la carte menu in a spectacular waterfront setting.

The hotel also prides itself on being able to create and customise dining experiences for any occasion. The staff will be pleased to arrange anything from sunset cocktails and beach banquets to a private meal in one's villa or a special celebration aboard a yacht.

The Labyrinth lounge is the perfect 'sundowner' location. It offers views of the lagoon and sea from sunken seats that give one the illusion of floating in the surrounding azure blue water while listening to live music.

The Elixir Spa offers a range of Ayurvedic therapies by trained Indian therapists, using local organic plants and extracts. There are also chocolate and honey massages, caviar anti-toxin therapy, and couple treatments in a private garden. Elixir also boasts an indoor pool, lounges and sauna, as well as a state-of-the-art cardio-fitness gym and beauty centre.

When all that pampering and relaxation get to be too much, there's golf, basketball, mini-football, watersports and tennis, in addition to the Grecoland kid's club for younger guests. Excursions to the Palace of Knossos and other local sights can also be arranged.

elounda bay palace

THIS PAGE: *Enjoy meals on the waterfront at 'F' Restaurant.*

OPPOSITE (FROM LEFT): *The Presidential Suite has its own private pool and offers views of the bay; soft king-sized beds and bright, airy décor characterise Elounda Bay Palace's luxury suites.*

Just like the gorgeous postcard vistas that the Greek islands are famous for, the Elounda Bay Palace is a beach resort surrounded by clear azure skies, deep blue water and white sand. The hotel is less than an hour's drive from Heraklion International Airport, minutes away from the museums and attractions of Agios Nikolaos, and a short stroll from the peaceful fishing town of Elounda.

A member of 'The Leading Hotels of the World', the resort embraces a full 8 hectares (20 acres) of landscaped greenery on the water's edge. It offers 244 guestrooms and suites, a private beach and sporting facilities, all overlooking the calm beauty of Mirabello Bay and the open sea. A watersports centre provides opportunities for scuba diving, windsurfing, fishing, and jet skiing under the warm Cretan sun. There is also a freshwater pool for children, an outdoor saltwater pool, and a temperature-controlled indoor pool.

With its wide panoramic windows, guests at the ThalaSpa Chenot enjoy sweeping views of the sea. Enjoy Chenot's renowned body and

...surrounded by clear azure skies, deep blue water, and white sand.

face treatments performed by highly trained therapists, who draw on their vast experience and a repertoire of signature Chenot massage techniques to suit the unique needs and desires of the individual guest.

To simplify the matter of choosing from the resort's catalogue of rooms, suites, bungalows, villas and penthouses, the hotel uses a system of five unique club categories. Smart Club rooms are located in the main building with either mountain- or sea-facing views, and include all the high-tech amenities and services—such as complimentary bottles of wine upon arrival—which have brought the property widespread acclaim.

The Prestige and Elite Club categories encompass a range of deluxe bungalows and family suites with access to shared heated pools. Silver Club villas have their own private heated pools directly on the edge of the sea.

For sheer opulence, however, little can compare to the Exclusive Club's offerings. A single Presidential Suite promises a superstar experience with floor-to-ceiling views of the bay from within, and a private pool bordering the water along a generous patio. Marble bathrooms, Bulgari toiletries, fireplaces and elegant furnishings complete the 80-sq-m (861-sq-ft) residence with a touch of class.

'F' Restaurant serves up tantalising modern cuisine that takes taste buds on a tour of the Mediterranean, combining vibrant flavours with verve and imagination. The Blue Lagoon Polynesian Restaurant & Sushi Bar takes one even farther away, while Greek favourites are always in bountiful supply at Aretoussa and the romantic Thalassa Restaurant.

Miles away from the cares of the world, this spectacular resort on Crete's Mirabello Bay waterfront has it all.

rooms
244 rooms and suites

food
Thalassa: seafood • Aretoussa: international • 'F': modern Mediterranean • Ariadne Taverna: grilled meats, fish and regional • Blue Lagoon Polynesian Restaurant & Sushi Bar: Polynesian • Argonaut Seaside Restaurant: fresh seafood and Italian • Dionyssos: Greek • Kafenion: Cretan

drink
Erato Lounge Bar • Poseidon Pool Bar • sail-in jetty bar

features
ThalaSpa Chenot • watersports • indoor and outdoor pools • landscaped gardens • 5 tennis courts • basketball and volleyball courts • games room • shops • conference rooms

nearby
Elounda village • Agios Nikolaos • museums • shops

contact
Elounda, Crete 72053 • telephone: +30.28410.67 000 • facsimile: +30.28410.41 783 • email: bay@eloundabay.gr • website: www.eloundabay.gr

elounda beach

*THIS PAGE: Yachting Club Villas
are built directly over the
water, the perfect choice for
an avid watersports fan.*
*OPPOSITE: Enjoy a drink at Veghera
Jetty Bar under the billowing
blue and white canopy.*

For nearly four decades now, a single spot on the northeastern coast of Crete has been admired for being a perfect convergence of sandy beach, sea views and Mediterranean climate. Elounda Beach is not only the name of the location, but also of the luxurious resort that has set the benchmark to which all others aspire and is responsible for the beach's sparkling reputation.

Established in 1971, Elounda Beach is constantly working to improve the experience that it offers its visitors. As such, it has recently launched its extraordinary Yachting Club Villas. Situated directly over the water,

these villas represent the zenith of modern resort luxury in the Mediterranean, providing a fitting backdrop as visitors escape to a world of exclusive relaxation. Boasting a striking architectural style that makes each residence resemble a billowing sail from afar, they proudly carry the marks of nautical influence throughout the design of their stunning interiors. All imaginable conveniences are provided to ensure that one's holiday experience is perfect in every way. The latest Blu-ray video equipment powers the villas' home theatre systems, and every aspect of the environment is controlled from a central touch panel. Heated indoor pools are lit with fibre optics and feature counter-current waves and hydromassage jets. On the lowest level of each villa lies a personal jet ski for adventurous guests, and a dining table for romantic meals by the water.

A member of 'The Leading Hotels of the World', Elounda Beach has been honoured on awards lists for almost as long as it has offered its quintessential Greek holiday experience. A staple of *Condé Nast Traveler* magazine's prestigious 'Gold List' for over 10 years, it has also been named one of Europe's best beach hotels (*Geo Saison*, January 2008) and 'Best of the Greek Islands' (Andrew Harper's *Hideaway Report*, 2003).

Travelling to the exclusive resort is a simple affair and involves just a 40-minute drive from Heraklion International Airport. To arrive in presidential style, consider booking a flight with the hotel's private jet service. Step onto the luxury aircraft at the nearest European airport, and prepare to be shuttled first-class to Heraklion, minus the delays, fixed schedules and rigid procedures that plague so much of modern air travel. In some cases, guests staying at the hotel's most prestigious accommodations may even enjoy the jet as a complimentary service.

Upon arrival, it's not hard to understand why international critics adore Elounda Beach so. The view over Mirabello Bay is almost too perfect to be real: blue skies with barely a hint of cloud cover and clear views across

sparkling water all the way to the island of Spinalonga across the gulf—all of it bathed in warm golden light during the day and intimate sunsets come evening.

With the variety of water activities and leisure facilities on offer, none of the hotel's beachside splendour goes to waste. A watersports centre provides all the training and equipment required for sailing out on the bay, jet and water skiing over the waves, or fishing on a boat surrounded by nothing but miles of open sea. The beach is a long stretch gently covered with fine white sand, a

screenings and a variety of live performances. Couples can enjoy the cool night air as they weave a romantic ambience under the stars.

Henri Chenot, the renowned provider of wellness treatments, has collaborated with Elounda Beach to create the ThalaSpa Chenot. Combining Henri Chenot's unique 'biontology' methods with thalassotherapy, the spa helps visitors create a menu of treatments to suit their individual needs. Using wraps, Chenot's signature massages and other aesthetic treatments, therapists revitalise guests and restore the energy that has been sapped through the rigours of daily life. The spa's treatments work best when combined with a meal from their Bio-light menu, which is full of innovative recipes that balance healthy eating with unforgettable flavours.

Equally effective in stripping away the cares of the world are the resort's 250 lavishly appointed guestrooms, suites and villas. These range from the rooms of the Comfort VIP Club, whose windows in the main building look out to either sea or garden-facing views, to the Platinum Club, where enormous standalone villas afford their occupants all the pleasures of a private residence on the edge of the Mediterranean. Every accommodation at Elounda Beach promises an unforgettable vacation. Each room comes equipped with video-on-demand channels, Internet access, CD/DVD players and bathrooms where features such as jacuzzis and steam baths are standard.

sunbather's dream indeed. Even after they return to the comfort of the hotel, guests may enjoy the pure Mirabello Bay seawater in a heated outdoor pool.

Land lovers warming up to the sea at their own pace will find plenty to do in the meantime. Tennis, basketball, badminton and volleyball courts are located on the premises. There is also a mini-golf course which is especially popular with families travelling with children. In the evenings, a large open-air amphitheatre becomes the stage for film

...all the pleasures of a private residence on the edge of the Mediterranean.

The Platinum Club's Palace Suite is a bold construction which takes everything that can be found in the 'high life' and improves upon it. The suite occupies a generous 360 sq m (3,875 sq ft) of space and includes two pools, five elegant bedrooms, six bathrooms, three living rooms, a kitchen, dining area and a private gym over two expansive bungalow suites. The welcome spread includes a bottle of Dom Perignon, which can be enjoyed leisurely during the in-suite check-in.

Elounda Beach has not only won accolades for its all-out approach to providing travellers with the finest in facilities, comforts and design—it is also renowned for serving up some of the best food on the Greek islands. Restaurants such as Dionyssos and the Blue Lagoon have been recognised by such publications as *Wine Spectator*, and have even received the prestigious Five Star Diamond Award. Traditional Greek cuisine is lovingly represented by a number of the hotel's eight restaurants, and one can also find fusion dishes, seafood and international specialities.

Elounda Beach has enchanted two generations of discerning clientele from all over the world. With its dedication to staying one step ahead of the times—clearly evident in the Yachting Club Villas—one can assume the next generation will be similarly charmed.

rooms
250 rooms, suites and villas

food
Argonaut Seaside Restaurant: fresh seafood and Italian • Blue Lagoon Polynesian Restaurant & Sushi Bar: Polynesian • Kafenion: Cretan • Aretoussa: international • Thalassa: seafood • 'F': Mediterranean • Ariadne Taverna: grilled meats, fish and regional • Dionyssos: Greek

drink
Veghera Jetty Bar • Lito: lobby bar • Neraida: pool bar • Beach Bar • sail-in jetty bar

features
ThalaSpa Chenot • watersports centre • pools • beach • landscaped gardens • tennis courts • volleyball and basketball courts • games room • mini-golf • amphitheatre • private jet and limousine service • wireless Internet access

nearby
Elounda • Agios Nιkolaos

contact
Elounda, 72053 Crete • telephone: +30.28410.63 000 • facsimile: +30.28410.41 373 • email: elohotel@eloundabeach.gr • website: www.eloundabeach.gr

minos beach art hotel

Few opportunities exist to allow travellers to experience how a country's artistic interpretations relate to her landscape. Perhaps, for that very reason, bluegr Mamikadis Hotels established the Minos Beach Art Hotel, an extraordinary showcase of art and sculptures from artists all over the world.

Located in the secluded Agios Nikolaos district of Crete, Minos Beach Art Hotel was named one of Greece's leading hotels in 2008 by the WTA. Guests staying here for any length of time will surely agree that the award was well-deserved. Consisting of waterfront bungalows built in the traditional style of Cretan architecture, each distinctive white structure exemplifies the region's close relationship with nature.

As the name suggests, Minos Beach Art Hotel's main attraction lies in its stunning collection of artwork. An important element of the hotel's aesthetic is its sculpture garden, an international collection comprising over 45 original works. Artists such as Abakanowicz, Borbas, Frangantonis and Varotsos—just to name a few—have contributed their own interpretations of Cretan vistas. Amidst cool olive trees and flowering bougainvilleas, the exhibition contains many site-specific pieces that mirror the peaceful locale. Installations are updated every alternate summer, so returning guests have something new to look forward to.

Rooms are furnished to five-star standards with modern conveniences such as in-room safes, direct-dial telephones and minibars.

THIS PAGE (FROM LEFT): The light décor scheme gives rooms a bright and spacious feeling; enjoy a range of watersports, or just sunbathe on the beach.

OPPOSITE (FROM LEFT): The restaurant La Bouillabaisse has tables by the water, so one can dine with views of the sea; the pristine bungalows are built in traditional Cretan style.

rooms
104 seafront rooms and bungalows, waterfront bungalows and villas • 25 Junior Suites

food
La Bouillabaisse: gourmet restaurant • Terpsis: Cretan • Ambrosia: international • Bacchus: international

drink
Dionyssos: cocktail bar • Ibiscus: pool bar • Pure: lounge bar

features
Ananea Spa • outdoor sculpture gallery • mini gym • conference room • TV lounge • watersports

nearby
Agios Nikolaos shopping centre • traditional village of Kritsa • Panagia Kera–Byzantine church • Spinalonga island • Knossos Palace • Lato archaeological site • Lassithi plateau

contact
Agios Nikolaos, 72100 Crete • telephone: +30.28410.22 345 • facsimile: +30.28410.22 548 • email: info-minos@bluegr.com • website: www.bluegr.com

Any of the 49 Superior Bungalows are highly recommended for couples looking to get away. For an extra-special vacation, book an Executive Villa. With beautifully furnished interiors and private pools by the water, these two-bedroom villas offer panoramic views, gorgeous en-suite facilities complete with jacuzzis and steam cabins, and living rooms of generous proportions.

The Presidential Villa is the standout choice for those who want only the best. Its master bedroom enjoys a spa bathroom, while two other rooms share another jacuzzi-equipped bathroom. Lounge around the private seafront pool while watching the soothing waves, and enjoy a swim at any time.

As with everything else it offers, the hotel doesn't disappoint when it comes to food. Dine by the water's edge with La Bouillabaisse,

a restaurant serving gourmet French cuisine. Terpsis, a traditional Greek taverna, celebrates the Cretan culinary art with barbecues and dance performances.

Given the setting and the stunningly clear waters surrounding the bungalows, it should come as no surprise that the hotel offers a range of exciting watersports and other aquatic activities. Professional scuba diving instruction and assistance are available for both beginners and confident divers, and beach towels are never in short supply for sunbathers. More relaxing still is Ananea Spa, named after the Greek word for renewal. From a menu of full-body treatments and Ayurvedic techniques, tired guests can find respite from stress and exhaustion. With any luck, they might even find the inspiration to create some art of their own.

out of the blue, capsis elite resort

THIS PAGE (FROM LEFT): *For utmost privacy and comfort, choose one of the maisonettes; the resort is situated on its own private peninsula.*

OPPOSITE (FROM LEFT): *The Black Pearl Residence is one of the resort's most exclusive suites; experienced therapists will help soothe aching muscles.*

One of the most environmentally progressive resorts in the Aegean Sea, Out of the Blue, Capsis Elite Resort sprawls across a private peninsula on the northern coast of Crete. Recently renovated, the luxury resort is ideally located for exploring Iraklion and nearby ancient sites such as the Palace of Knossos.

Winner of the Worldwide Hospitality Award 2002 for 'Best Innovation in Terms of Environmental Protection' as well as the 2008 Star Diamond Award, the resort comprises almost 17 hectares (41 acres) of parkland and gardens with subtropical plants, meandering paths, marble statues, waterfalls, lily ponds and gorgeous sea views. The grounds also boast organic greenhouses, orchards and fields, where much of the produce used at the resort's restaurants is grown.

The Cladissos River flows through the northern part of the gardens on its final leg to the sea, and around the edge of the park are three beaches, a private zoo and the Minoan amusement park with its family-friendly games, tree houses and lagoon-style pool. If that's not enough to keep guests busy, the resort also offers a range of activities such as watersports, an aqua park and tennis. Last but not least, the Euphoria Rejuvenating Spa offers total relaxation with a menu of holistic treatments and therapies that don't just focus on external appearances.

The accommodation is designed to resemble a Cretan village and includes five distinct elements: three hotels and three 'neighbourhoods' with suites, bungalows, villas and maisonettes with private pools.

Unveiled in 2008, the resort's latest addition is the Crystal Energy Hotel, which overlooks the St Athanasios Chapel, Aghia Pelaghia village and Cladissos Bay. Located in the centre of the complex, the hotel offers a

unique Fit 4 Life Fitness Lounge. The two- and three-bedroom suites feature modern décor and cosy atmospheres with great views.

Perfect for couples in search of a romantic getaway, the Ruby Red Regal Hotel has its own reception, a private freshwater pool, gourmet restaurant and other adult-only amenities—to maintain an intimate atmosphere, children under 10 years old are not accepted. Public areas feature Greek marble, antique furniture and fixtures influenced by Minoan designs. Paintings by famous Greek artists adorn the walls and harmonise with Cretan touches.

The Eternal Oasis neighbourhood is wedged between the gardens and Cladissos Bay. The bungalows and maisonettes are decorated with a blend of European panache and Cretan flair—dramatic black-and-white floor tiles accented with Busnelli furniture and a background of earth tones. The VIP Divine Thalassa neighbourhood offers seafront suites, maisonettes and villas. The romantic junior suites feature elegant Italian Boffi Collection furnishings and sumptuous black marble bathrooms. Maisonettes boast private pools and gardens, with furnishing and fixtures that offer luxury without pretension.

The utmost in privacy and luxury can be found at the Oh! All-Suite Hotel. The exclusive compound features a separate entrance and its facilities—restaurants, pool, spa and private beach—are only available to Oh! guests.

rooms
465 suites, bungalows, maisonettes and villas

food
Precieux Gourmet Restaurant • Safran Italian Restaurant • El Greco Gourmet Restaurant • Knossos Private Restaurant • H2O Aqua Fusion Restaurant • Red Pepper Mediterranean Restaurant • Raki Cretan Restaurant • Musses Private Pool Restaurant • Poseidon Fish Taverna • Aqua Marine Beach Restaurant

drink
Precieux Bar • Ikaros Lobby Bar • Azure Pool Bar • Aqua Marine Beach Bar • Euphoria Rejuvenating Spa Bar • Hot Spot Bar • Dazzle Disco Bar • Blue Diva Bar

features
Euphoria Rejuvenating Spa • Minoan amusement park • pools • beaches • gym • watersports • tennis • billiards • shops • zoo • wireless Internet • heliport • business centre

nearby
golf • horse riding • water park • aquarium • bird watching • shopping • nightlife • archaeological sites and museum

contact
Aghia Pelaghia, Heraklion, 75100 Crete • telephone: +30.2810.811 112 • facsimile: +30.2810.811 076 • email: reservation@capsis.gr • website: www.capsis.com

corfu imperial

Perched on a lushly wooded peninsula with pristine sea on either side, the Corfu Imperial recalls the days when the Ionian Isles were an exclusive, warm-weather retreat for the rich and royal from around Europe.

From the moment one steps into the lobby—still with its original frescoes, crystal chandeliers and classical furnishings—one is transported back to the era when Queen Victoria of England and Empress Sisi of Austria spent their summers relaxing and socialising with other aristocrats on the island.

All accommodation at the Corfu Imperial is dressed in the very finest fabrics and furnishings, as well as parquet floors, while huge picture windows and private balconies provide magnificent views. Bungalows are nestled in the gardens, providing an oasis of peace, with some offering private terraces and direct beach access. Suites run the gamut from petite studios to spacious one-bedroom apartments, all individually furnished with handmade *objets d'art* and antiques. The ultra-chic Palazzo villas boast their own yacht moorings and private pools.

The two-bedroom Palazzo Imperiale occupies its own mini peninsula, with the pool deck connecting to a secluded sandy cove. Decorated in the Italian regency style, the villa offers a seamless transition between indoor and outdoor living. A fully equipped kitchen affords the option of privately catered meals, while the master bathroom features a 'river bath' large enough for two, complete with views of the sea.

The variety of accommodation is matched only by the sumptuous dining options available at the resort. The Imperial Corfu's signature Aristos gourmet restaurant was named after Greek shipping tycoon Aristotle Onassis, who once owned the nearby Scorpios Island. Elegant décor, silver and crystal table settings, outstanding service and a lavish menu designed by executive chef Michael Rougas promises a memorable experience for all diners.

THIS PAGE: All rooms are fitted with the finest furniture, and have lovely views from picture windows and private balconies.

OPPOSITE (FROM LEFT): The Palazzo Imperiale villa recalls the opulence of Italy's regency days; seen from above, the Corfu Imperial is surrounded by lush forests and sparkling water.

rooms
301 suites, palazzos and dream villas

food
Aristos: gourmet international •
Poolside Restaurant: casual • Yali: fusion •
Mon Repos: Mediterranean • Nafsika:
Mediterranean brassiere

drink
Odysseus lounge bar • Alkinoos Lobby bar •
Yali beach bar

features
Elixir Spa • Grecoland kids' club • indoor and
outdoor pools •3 beaches • fitness club with
gym • tennis courts • windsurfing •
waterskiing • sailing • bikes • cultural shows

nearby
Corfu Town • Kanoni Island • National Art
Gallery • traditional villages • golf • horseback
riding • tavernas

contact
PO Box 306, 49100 Kommeno, Corfu •
telephone: +30.26610.88 400 •
facsimile: +30.26610.91 881 •
email: sales_ci@grecotel.gr •
website: www.corfuimperial.com

Yali specialises in fresh seafood prepared in imaginative ways and accompanied by fine champagne. Mon Repos offers an astounding variety of hot and cold Mediterranean dishes together with sweeping views of the Ionian Sea. Situated by the pool, the Odysseus lounge bar is the perfect place to watch the setting sun or while away a few evening hours with cocktails and live music.

Besides lazing by the water, the Imperial Corfu offers a host of activities such as watersports, tennis courts and cycling. Its facilities include a gymnasium, a Grecoland kids' club, and a library salon stocked with music and games. Guests can also partake of nearby golf and horseback riding.

The resort is near Corfu Town, with a twice daily bus service from the lobby to the town centre. For those who feel like stretching their legs in the evening, there are a few local tavernas within a 10-minute walk.

The stunning Elixir Spa—with its glass walls and indoor 'goddess' pool—is the perfect place to de-stress or enjoy customised beauty treatments rendered with Carita cosmetics. The 'Imperial Garden Elixir' promises to detoxify, combat cellulite and obesity, and speed up the metabolism while toning and moisturising. The 'Imperial Massage' includes total body aromatherapy, drainage massage, head and face massage, as well as shiatsu and reflexology on the extremities.

index

index

index

index

picturecredits+acknowledgements

The publisher would like to thank the following for permission to reproduce their photographs:

AFP/Getty Images 102
Alamer -/Photolibrary 27 (bottom)
alexandr6868/iStockphoto 90 (top)
Allan Baxter /Getty Images 55, 19, 23 (bottom), front cover (statues)
Alpha Estate 108–109
Alvaro Leiva/Photolibrary 43 (bottom)
Amirandes 136–137, 150–151
Angelo Cavalli/Getty Images 23 (top), 46, front flap (temple) 121 (bottom)
Angelo Cavalli/Photolibrary 12
Aris Messinis/AFP/Getty Images 5,16, back cover (statue), 28, 31 (top), 41 (middle), 79, 81 (bottom)
Astrolavos Art Galleries 29 (bottom)
Athens Life Gallery 56–57
Belvedere Hotel 36 (top), 128–129, front cover (bowl)
Bilderbuch -/Photolibrary 25 (bottom)
Bob Thomas/Popperfoto/Getty Images 48 (top)
Brian MacDonald Photography -/Photolibrary 33 (top)
Bridgeman Art Library/Getty Images 21 (bottom)
Chris Caldicott/Getty Images 90 (bottom)
Christopher and Sally Gable/Getty Images 30
Classical 2, Fashion House Hotel 58–59, front cover (shoes)
Classical BabyGrand Hotel 32, 60–61, back cover (dress) back flap (ostrich)
Classical King George Palace 62–63, front flap (artwork)
Corfu Imperial 148–149
crowman/iStockphoto 124

David Sanger/Getty Images 42 (bottom)
David Silverman/Getty Images 39 (bottom right)
De Agostini/Getty Images 25 (top)
Domaine Gerovassiliou 40, 110–111
Elounda Bay Palace 138–139
Elounda Beach 140–143, front cover (villa exterior)
Emilio Suetone/Getty Images 34 (top)
Emmanouil Filippou/iStockphoto 125, 127
Estate Hatzimichalis 94–95
Fayez Nureldine/AFP/Getty Images 15, 99 (bottom), back cover (horse)
Filippo Monteforte/AFP/Getty Images 41 (bottom)
Frank & Helen Schreider/National Geographic/Getty Images 26 (bottom)
Frank Krahmer/Getty Images 2, 116, front cover (steps)
Fred Derwal/Getty Images 21 (top)
Georg Gerster/Photolibrary 17
Grand Resort Lagonissi 36 (bottom), 64–65
Grecotel Cape Sounio 66–67
Greg Johnston/Getty Images 54
Guy Vanderelst/Getty Images 8–9
Hasan Mroue/AFP/Getty Images 81 (top)
Hermann Erber/LOOK-foto/Getty Images 89
Hervé Gyssels/Photolibrary 103
Hilton Athens 33, 68–69
Holly Harris/Getty Images 45 (bottom)
Hugh Sitton/Getty Images 120
Imaret 106–107
Ingolf Pompe/Photolibrary 43 (middle)
Island Club + Restaurant 70–71
Jack Hollingsworth/Photolibrary 14

James Sparshatt/Getty Images 51 (bottom), back cover (guards)
Jamie Baker/Getty Images 121 (top)
Jamie McDonald/Getty Images 48 (bottom)
JTB Photo/Photolibrary 100
Katja Kreder/Getty Images 27 (top left), 37 (top)
Kir-Yianni 112–113, back cover (vineyard)
Ktima Biblia Chora 41 (top), 114–115
Liana Vourakis 29 (middle)
Louis-Laurent Grandadam/Getty Images 20, 22 (bottom)
Lousia Gouliamaki/AFP/Getty Images 13, back cover (plane), 29 (top), 39 (top), 50, back cover (graffiti), 101 (top)
Luca Trovato/Getty Images 123
Marco Simoni/Getty Images 122
Mark Hannaford/Photolibrary 76, back cover (canal)
Marvin E. Newman/Getty Images 27 (top right)
Michael Tullberg/Getty Images 43 (top)
Milos Bicanski/Getty Images 1, 42 (top)
Minos Beach Art Hotel 144–145
Mykonos Blu 130–131, front cover (donkey), front cover (interior)
Nafplia Palace Hotel + Suites 84–86
Nicholas Pitt/Getty Images 44, front cover (beach)
Out of the Blue, Capsis Elite Resort 146–147
Perivolas 6, 134–135
Pete Turner/Getty Images 4
Peter Adams/Getty Images 82
Photo Researchers/Photolibrary 91
photoposter/iStockphoto 93

RB.M.PhotoArt /Photolibrary 83
Rene Mattes/Photolibrary 22 (top)
Richard Nowitz/Getty Images 24
Robert Antansovski/AFP/Getty Images 51 (top)
Robert Harding/Photolibrary 31 (bottom)
Santa Marina Resort + Villas 132–133
Simeone Huber/Getty Images 52–53
Spondi 35, 37 (bottom)
Stephen Frink/Getty Images 45 (top)
Steve Outram/Getty Images 119
Steve Outram/Photolibrary 31 (middle)
Terrance Klassen/Photolibrary 105
The Print Collector/Photolibrary 39 (bottom left)
Thessaloniki Film Festival 99 (top)
Todd Korol/Aurora/Getty Images 53 (bottom), back flap (monk)
Tolo Balaguer/Photolibrary 86, 92, 104
t-palace @ Classical King George Palace 72–73
Travel Ink/Getty Images 101 (bottom)
Walter Bibikow/Getty Images 80, 96
Walter Bibikow/Photolibrary 34 (bottom), 38
Werner Otto/Photolibrary 26 (top)
Yoray Liberman/Getty Images 45 (middle)
Yorgos Matthaios/EB via Getty Images 18 (bottom)
Yvan Travert/Photolibrary 126
Zoumboulakis Galleries 74–75

The publisher would like to thank Mr Andreas Goros, Mrs Maria Makri, Josephine Pang and Jocelyn Lau for their help and support during the production of this book.

ATHENS + GREATER ATTICA

HOTELS

Athens Life Gallery
103 Thisseos Avenue, Ekali
Athens 14578
telephone: +30 .210. 626 0400
facsimile: • +30 .210. 622 9353
email: info-lifegallery@bluegr.com
website: www.bluegr.com

Classical 2, Fashion House Hotel
2 Pireos Street, Athens 10552
telephone: +30.210.523 5230
facsimile: +30.210.523 4955
email: 2fhh@classicalhotels.com
website: www.classicalhotels.com

Classical BabyGrand Hotel
65 Athinas & Lycourgou Street
Athens 10551
telephone: +30.210.325 0900
facsimile: +30.210.325 0920
email: bg@classicalhotels.com
website: www.classicalhotels.com

Classical King George Palace
3 Vasileos Georgiou 1st Street, Syntagma Square
Athens 10564
telephone: +30.210.322 2210
facsimile: +30.210.325 0504
email: kgpalace@classicalhotels.com
website: www.classicalhotels.com

Grand Resort Lagonissi
40th Km Athens-Sounion Avenue
19010 Lagonissi, Athens, Greece
telephone: +30.22910.76 000
facsimile: +30.22910.24 534
email: reservations@grandresort.gr
website: www.grandresort.gr

Grecotel Cape Sounio
67 km Athens–Sounio Road, GR-195
Sounio Attica
telephone: +30.2292.069 700
facsimile: +30.2292.069 770
email: reserv_so@grecotel.gr
website: www.capesounio.com

Hilton Athens
46 Vassilisis Sofias Avenue,
Athens 11528
telephone: +30.210.728 1000
facsimile: +30.210.728 1111
email: pr.athens@hilton.com
website: www.hiltonathens.gr

RESTAURANTS

Island Club + Restaurant
27th km of Athens–Sounio Avenue, Sounio Attica
telephone: +30.210.965 3563 / +30.210.965 3564
telephone: +30.210.892 5053
website: www.islandclubrestaurant.gr

Island Art & Taste (banquets and conferences)
telephone: +30.210.892 5000
facsimile: +30.210.892 5050
email: sales@panasgroup.gr
website: www.islandartandtaste.gr/www.panasgroup.gr

T-Palace at Classical King George Palace
3 Vassileos Georgiou 1st Street, Syntagma Square,
Athens 10564
telephone: +30.210.322 2210
facsimile: +30.210.325 0504
website: www.classicalhotels.com

GALLERIES

Zoumboulakis Galleries
20 Kolonaki Square, Athens 10673
telephone: +30.210.360 8278
facsimile: +30.210.363 1364
email: galleries@zoumboulakis.gr

7 Kriezotou Street, Athens 10671
telephone: +30.210.363 1951
facsimile: +30.210.362 9980
email: kriezoutou7@zoumboulakis.gr

6 Kriezotou Street, Athens 10671
telephone: +30.210.364 0264
facsimile: +30.210.364 3496
email: kriezoutou6@zoumboulakis.gr

37 Agathodemonos and 1 Orestrou Street
(off 199 Piraeus Street), Athens
telephone: +30.210.341 4214

website: www.zoumboulakis.gr/ www.zone-d.gr

PELOPONNESE

HOTELS

Nafplia Palace Hotel + Villas
Akronaflia, Nafplion,
Peloponnese 21100
telephone: +30.275.207 0800
facsimile: +30.275.202 8783
email: reservations@nafplionhotels.gr
website: www.nafplionhotels.gr

CENTRAL GREECE

VINEYARDS

Estate Hatzimichalis
Estate Hatzimichalis, c/o Demeter S. A.
13th km Athens-Lamia National Road
N Kifisia 14564
telephone: +30.210.807 6705-6
facsimile: +30.210.807 6704
email: info@hatzimichalis.gr
website: www.hatzimichalis.gr

NORTHERN GREECE

HOTELS

Imaret
30-32 Th Poulidou Street, Kavala
telephone: +30.2510.620 151
facsimile: +30.2510.620 156
email: info@imaret.gr
website: www.imaret.gr

VINEYARDS

Alpha Estate
2nd Km Amyndeon—Ag Panteleimonas
Amyndeon, Florina 53200
telephone: +30.238.602 0111
facsimile: +30.238.602 0132
email: info@alpha-estate.com
website: www.alpha-estate.com

Domaine Gerovassiliou
Epanomi, Thessaloniki 57500
telephone: +30.239.204 4567
facsimile: +30.239.204 4560
email: ktima@gerovassiliou.gr
website: www.gerovassiliou.gr

Kir-Yianni
Yianakohori, Naoussa 59200
telephone: +30.233.205 1100
facsimile: +30.233.205 1140
email: info@kiryianni.gr
website: www.kiryianni.gr

Ktima Biblia Chora
Kokkinochori, Kavala 64008
telephone: +30.25920.44 974
facsimile: +30.25920.44 975
email: ktima@bibliachora.gr
website: www.bibliachora.gr

ISLAND GREECE

HOTELS

Hotel Belvedere
School of Fine Arts District
84 600 Mykonos, Greece
telephone: +30.2289.025 122
facsimile: +30.2289.025 126
email: contact@belvederehotel.com
website: www.belvederehotel.com

Mykonos Blu
Psarou, Mykonos 84600
telephone: +30.2289.027 900
facsimile: +30.2289.027 783
e-mail: sales_mb@grecotel.gr
website: www.mykonosblu.com

Santa Marina Resort + Villas
Ornos Bay, Mykonos 84600
telephone: +30.228.902 3220
facsimile: +30.228.902 3412
email: info@santa-marina.gr
website: www.santa-marina.gr

Perivolas
Oia, Santorini 84702
telephone: +30.2286.071 308
facsimile: +30.2286.071 309
email: info@perivolas.gr
website: www.perivolas.gr

Amirandes
P.O. Box 106, GR-711 10, Iraklion
telephone: +30.2897.041 104
facsimile: +30.2897.041 113
email: sales_am@grecotel.gr
website: www.amirandes.com

Elounda Bay Palace
Elounda, Crete 72053
telephone: +30.28410.670 00
facsimile: +30.28410.417 83
email: bay@eloundabay.gr
website: www.eloundabay.gr

Elounda Beach
Elounda, Crete 72053
telephone: +30.28410.630 00
facsimile: +30.28410.413 73
email: elohotel@eloundabeach.gr
website: www.eloundabeach.gr

Minos Beach Art Hotel
Aghios Nikolaos, Crete
telephone: +30.284.102 2345
facsimile: +30.284.102 2548
email: info-minos@bluegr.com
website: www.bluegr.com

Out of the Blue, Capsis Elite Resort
Aghia Pelaghia, Heraklion, 75100 Crete
telephone: +30.210.614 9563
facsimile: +30.210.614 2072
email: reservation@capsis.gr
website: www.capsis.com

Corfu Imperial
P.O. Box 306, GR 49100, Kommeno, Corfu
telephone +30.2661.088 400
facsimile: +30.2661.091 881
email: sales_ci@grecotel.gr
website: www.corfuimperial.com

A CULTURAL LEGACY

Aghia Ekaterini
Chairefontos, Lysikratous, Galanou & Goura streets,
Plaka, Athens

Ancient Olympia Museum + Archaeological site
Olympia, Greece
telephone +30.26240.22 529
email: info@olympia-greece.org
website: www.Olympia-Greece.org

Ancient Pylos (Nestor's Palace) + Museum
Pylos, 4 km (2 mi) South of Chora 24001
telephone: +30.0763.31 358

Antivouniotissa Byzantine Museum
Arseniou Street, Kerkyra 49100
telephone +30.26610.38 313
facsimile: +30.26610.38 313

Arachaeological Museum of Rhodes
Megalou Alexandrou Square, Rhodes 85100
telephone: +30.22410.75 674/+30.22410.34 719
facsimile: +30.22410.31 048
email: protocol@kbepka.culture.gr

Archaeological Museum in Argostoli
G. Vergoti Street, Argostoli, Kefalonia 28100
telephone: +30.26710.28 300

Archaeological Museum in Sparta
71, Osiou Nikonos Street , Sparti, Lakdemona 23100
telephone.: +30.27310.28 575
facsimile: +30.27310.21 516

directory

Archaeological Museum of Corfu
1 Armeni Vraila Street, Corfu 49100
telephone: +30.26610.30 680
facsimile: +30.26610.43 452

Archaeological Museum of Herakleion
Xanthoudidou Street and Xatzidaki, Herakleion 71202
telephone: +30.2810.279 086/+30.2810.279 000
facsimile: +30.2810.279 071
email: amh@culture.gr

Archaeological Museum of Paros
Parikia, Paros 84400
telephone: +30.22840.21 231

Archaeological Museum of Pella
Thessaloniki-Edessa national highway, Pella, Macedonia 58005
telephone: +30.23820.31 160/+30.23820.31 278
facsimile: +30.23820.31 160

Jewish History Centre of Thessaloniki
24 Tsimiski Street, Thessaloniki 54624
telephone: +30.2310.227 9063/+30.2310.223 231
facsimile: +30.2310.279 063/+30.2310.223 231

Archaeological Museum of Vathy
Vathy, Samos 83100
telephone: +30.22730.27 469

Archaeological Museum of Volos
1 Athanasaki Street, Volos, 38001
telephone: +30.24210.25285
facsimile: +30.24210.28563

Archaeological Museum of Thebes
Threpsiadou 1, Plateia Keramopoulou, Thiva, Viotia 32200
telephone: +30.22620.27 913
facsimile: +30.22620.23 559

Benaki Museum
Koubari 1 & Vasilissis Sofias, Syntagma, Athens
telephone: +30.210.367 1000
facsimile: +30.210.367 1063
email: benaki@benaki.gr
website: www.benaki.gr

Church of Panaghia Kapnikarea
Ermou & Kapnikareas Streets
Syntagma, Monastiraki, Athens

Church of Panagia Parigoritissa
Arta 47100
telephone: +30.26510.25 989
facsimile: +30.26510.39 349

Epigraphical Museum
1 Tosita Street, Athens 10682
telephone: +30.210.832 950/+30.210.821 7637
facsimile: +30.210.822 5133

Fethiye Mosque
Panos & Pelopida streets, Athens

Goulandris Museum of Cycladic and Ancient Greek Art
4 Neophytou Douka Street, Athens 10674
telephone: +30.210.722 8321 - 3
facsimile: +30.210.723 9382
email: info@cycladic-m.gr
website: www.cycladic-m.gr/

Hadrian's Gate
Amalias Avenue, Athens

Ilias Lalaounis Jewelry Museum
12 Kallisperi & Karyatidon streets, Acropolis, Athens 11742
telephone: +30.210.922 1044
facsimile: +30.210.923 7358
email: info@lalaounis-jewelrymuseum.gr
website: www.lalaounis-jewelrymuseum.gr

Islamic Art Museum
22 Ag. Asomaton & 12 Dipilou Street, Athens 10674
telephone: +30.210.325 1311
facsimile: +30.210.322 5550
email: islamic_collection@benaki.gr
website: www.benaki.gr

Jewish History Centre of Thessaloniki
24 Tsimiski Street, Thessaloniki 54624
telephone: +30.2310.227 9063/+30.2310.223 231
facsimile: +30.2310.279 063/+30.2310.223 231

Jewish Museum
Nikis 39, Syntagma, Athens 10557
telephone: +30.210.322 5582
facsimile: +30.210. 323 1577
email: info@jewishmuseum.gr
website: www.jewishmuseum.gr

Kerameikos Museum
Ermou 148, Thissio, Athens 10553
telephone: +30.210.346 3552

Lysicrates Monument
Lysicratous Square & Tripodon Street, Plaka, Syntagma, Athens

Marathon Archaeological Museum
114 Plataion Street, Marathon 19007
telephone: +30.22940.551 55

Municipal Museum, Castle of Ioannina
Ioannina, Epirus
Tel.+30.26510.26 356

Museum of Asian Art
Palea Anactora - Spianada, Corfu 49100
telephone: +30.26610.30 443/+30.26610.20 193
facsimile: +30.26610.81932
email: mast@culture.gr

Museum of Byzantine Culture
2 Stratou Avenue, Thessaloniki 54640
telephone: +30.2310.868 570
facsimile: +30.2310.838 597
email: mbp@culture.gr
website: www.mbp.gr/html/gr/index.htm

Museum of Contemporary Art
Kallirois Avenue & Am. Frantzi Street, Athens 11743
telephone: +30.210.924 2111-2
facsimile: +30.210.924 5200,
e-mail: protocol@emst.gr
website: www.emst.gr

Museum of Greek Folk Art
17 Kydathinaio, Plaka, Syntagma, Athens 10558
telephone: +30.210.322 9031
facsimile: +30.210.322 6979
email: melt@melt.culture.gr

Museum of Greek Musical Instruments
1-3 Diogenous Street, Athens
Telephone: +30.210.325 0198

Museum of the Ancient Agora
Adrianou 24, Athens 10550
telephone: +30.210.321 0185

Museum of the City of Athens
Paparrigopoulou 5-7, Panepistimio, Athens 10561
telephone: +30.210.323 1397
facsimile: +30.210.322 0765
website: www.athenscitymuseum.gr/

Museum of the Olive and Greek Olive Oil
129 Othonos–Amalias Streeet, Sparta, 23100
telephone: +30.27310.89 315
facsimile: +30.27310.89 325
email: piop@piraeusbank.gr
website: www.piop.gr

Mycenae Archaeological Museum
Mykines (Prefecture of Argolida)
telephone: +30.27510.76 585/+30.27510.76 802

Napflio Archaeological Museum
Plateia Syntagma (Constitution Square), Nafplion
telephone: +30.27520.27 502

National Archaeological Museum
44 Patission Street, Athens 11257
telephone: +30.210.821 7724
facsimile: +30.210.821 3573/+30.210.823 0800
email: eam@culture.gr

New Acropolis Museum
2-4 Makryianni Street, Athens 11742
telephone: +30.210.924 1043
facsimile: +30.210.924 1643
email: oanmapr@oanma.gr
website: www.newacropolismuseum.gr/eng/

Numismatic Museum
Panepistimiou 12, Syntagma, Athens 10671
telephone: +30.210.364 3774
facsimile: +30.210.363 5953
email: protocol@nm.culture.gr
website: www.nma.gr

Panagia Gorgoepikoos
Mitropoleos Square, Athens 10030

Panathenaic Stadium
Arditos Hill, Athens
telephone: +30.210.325 1744

Peloponnesian Folklore Foundation
V. Alexandrou 1, Nafplion, Argolis 21100
telephone: +30.27520.28 947
facsimile: +30.27520.27 960
email: pff@otenet.gr

Piraeus Archaeological Museum
31, Charliaou Trikoupi Street, Piraeus 18536
telephone: +30.210.452 1598/+30.210.4518 388

Roman Agora + Tower of the Winds
Corner of Eolou & Pepopida streets, Athens
telephone: +30.210.324 5220

Sotira Lykodemou
Od. Filellinon, Athens

Temple of Olympian Zeus
Vasilissis Olgas & Amalias, Acropolis, Athens
telephone: +30.210.922 6330

The acropolis of Athens
telephone: +30.210.321 0219

The Ancient Agora
Monastiraki, Thissio, Athens 11800
telephone: +30.210.321 0185

The Bath House of the Winds
8, Kyrristou street, Plaka, Athens
telephone: +30.210.322 9031

The National Gallery
1 Michalakopoulou Street & 50 Vas. Konstantinou Street, Athens 11528
telephone: +30.210.723 5857
facsimile: +30.210.722 4889
website: www.nationalgallery.gr

The Parthenon
Acropolis, Athens
telephone: +30.210.321 4172

Tzidarakis Mosque
Areos 1, Monastiraki Square, Athens
telephone: +30.210.324 2066

MADE IN GREECE

Alexandra
18 Sokratous Street, Corfu Town 49100

Angelo
120 Adrianou Street, Plaka, Athens

Antiqua
2 Amalias Avenue, Athens 10557
telephone: +30.210.323 2220
facsimile: +30.210.322 8304
web: http://www.antiqua.gr

Aristokratikón
9 Karagiórgi Servias, Syntagma, Athens 10563
telephone: +30.210.322 0546/+30.210.325 5649
facsimile: +30.210.360 3784
website: www.aristokratikon.com

Astrolavos Art Galleries
11 Irodotou Street, Kolonaki, Athens 10674
telephone: +30.210.722 1200-4
facsimile: +30.210.722 1304

Xanthippou 11, Kolonaki 10675
telephone: +30.210.729 4342-3
facsimile: +30.210.729 3317

email: gallery@astrolavos.gr
website: www.astrolavos.gr/

Bettina boutique
29 Anagnostopoulou & 40 Pindarou streets, Kolonaki, Athens 10673
telephone: +30.210.339 2094
facsimile: +30.210.339 2082
email: boutique@bettina.com.gr
website: www.bettina.com.gr

Bulgari
8 Voukourestiou Street, Athens 10564
website: www.bulgari.com

Donopoulos International Fine Arts
56 Andreou Georgiou Street, Thessaloniki 54627
telephone: +30.2310.552 633
email: ifa@donopoulos.gr
website: www.donopoulos.gr

Elena Votsi
7 Xanthou Street, Kolonaki, Athens
telephone: +30.210.360 0936
facsimile: +30.210.721 4768
email: ev@elenavotsi.com
website: www.elenavotsi.com

Gallery Nees Morfes
9 Valaoritou Street, Kolonaki, Athens 10671
telephone: +30.210.361 6165
facsimile: +30.210.363 7233
email: info@neesmorfesgallery.gr
website: www.neesmorfesgallery.gr

Green Farm
13 Dimokritou Street, Kolonaki, Athens
telephone: +30.210.364 001
facsimile: +30.210.361 4311
email: medfarm@otenet.gr
website: www.greenfarm.gr

Ilias Lalaounis
Kallisperi 12 & Karyatidon Street, Acropolis, Athens 11742
+30.210.922 1044,
facsimile: +30.210.923 7358
email: info@lalaounis-jewelrymuseum.gr
website: www.lalaounis-jewelrymuseum.gr.

6 Panepistimiou Street, Athens
telephone: +30.210.361 1371
email: info@lalaounis.gr
website: www.lalaounis.gr

Katerina Psoma
www.katerinapsoma.com

Kessaris
7 Panapistimiou Street, Athens 10564
telephone: +30.210.323 2919
website: www.kessaris.gr

Komboloi Museum Shop
25 Staikopoulou Street, Nafplion, Argolida 21100
telephone: +30.27520.21 618
facsimile: +30.27520.21 618
email: komuseum@otenet.gr
website: www.komboloi.gr

Kostas Antoniou
Ayiou Ioannou Street, Fira, Santorini
telephone: +30.22860.22 633
mobile: +30.6944.322 874
email: antoniouk@otenet.gr
website: antoniou.santorini.net

Loumidis Papagalos
106 Alolou Street at Panepistimiou Street, Athens
telephone: +30.210.321 6665
website: www.loumidisfoods.com

Michalis Aslanis
Lefkados 2b & Artis streets, Moschato, Athens 18346
telephone: +30.210.520 0552
facsimile: +30.210.520 1878
email: info@aslanishome.gr
website: www.aslanishome.gr

Ministry of Culture Museum Reproduction Shop
Ipitou Street, Old Town, Rhodes

Nikos & Takis
26 Skoufa Street, Kolonaki, Athens 10673
telephone: +30.210.331 0572
website: www.nikos-takis.com

Oino-Pnévmata
9a Irakleitou Street, Kolonaki, Athens 10673

Patounis Soap Factory
Ioanni Theotokis Street, Corfu Town 49100
telephone: +30.26610.39 806

Royal Oriental Carpets
33 Apellou Street Old Town, Rhodes
telephone: +30.22410.21 912

33 N.Nikodemou Street, Plaka, Athens 10558
telephone: +30.210.325 2822/+30.210.324 0537

email: info@orientalcarpet.gr
website: www.orientalcarpet.gr

Souzos
42, Guilford St, Corfu Town 49100
telephone: +30.26610.33 942
email: souzosfamily@acn.gr

Zolotas
10 Panepistimiou Street, Kolonaki, Athens 10671
telephone: +30.210.360 1272
facsimile: +30.210.361 3782

9 Stadiou Avenue Athens 10562
telephone: +30.210.322 1222
facsimile: +30.210.331 3320

website: www.zolotas.gr

Zoumboulakis Galleries
20 Kolonaki Square, Athens 10673
telephone: +30.210.360 8278
facsimile: +30.210.363 1364
email: galleries@zoumboulakis.gr

7 Kriezotou Street, Athens 10671
telephone: +30.210.363 1951
facsimile: +30.210.362 9980
email: kriezotou7@zoumboulakis.gr

6 Kriezotou Street, Athens 10671
telephone: +30.210.364 0264
facsimile: +30.210.364 3496
email: kriezotou6@zoumboulakis.gr

37 Agathodemonos and 1 Orestrou Street
(off 199 Piraeus Street), Athens
telephone: +30.210.341 4214

website: www.zoumboulakis.gr/www.zone-d.gr

EPICUREAN GREECE

Aegli Garden Restaurant
23 Kapodistriou Street, Corfu Town, 49100
telephone: +30.26610.319 49

Archaion Gefsis
22 Kodratou Street, Plateia Karaiskaki, Metaxourgeio,
Omonia Square, Athens
telephone: +30.210.523 9661

Aristotelis
8 Aristotelous Street, Thessaloniki
telephone: +30.2310.230 762

Avalon
20 Leokoriou Street, Psirri, Athens 10554
telephone: +30.210.331 0572

Blue Ginger
Argyraina - Mykonos 84600
telephone: +30.22890.27602
website: www.blueginger.gr

Blue Lagoon
Elounda, Crete 72053
telephone: +30.28410.63 000
facsimile: +30.28410.41 373
email: elohotel@eloundabeach.gr
website: www.eloundabeach.gr

Bokos
143 Maiandrou Street, Nea Ionia, Volos

Central (Central Funky Restaurant)
14 Filikis Etairias Square, Kolonaki, Athens 10673
telephone: +30.210.724 1059/+30.210.724 5938
facsimile: +30.210.722 9646
website: www.centralfunkyrestaurant.gr

Cubanita Habana
28 Karaeskaki Street, Psirri, Athens 10553
telephone: +30.210.331 4605
facsimile: +30.210.331 4608
email: mail@cubanita.gr
website: www.cubanita.gr

Dakos
6 Tsakalof Street, Kolonaki, Athens
telephone: +30.210.360 4020

Dionyssos
Elounda, Crete 72053
telephone: +30.28410.67 000
facsimile: +30.28410.41 783
email: bay@eloundabay.gr
website: www.eloundabay.gr

Dioskouri
16 D. Vasiliou Street, Neo Psihiko, Athens
telephone: +30.210.671 3997

Domata
Sani Resort Complex, Sani, Chalchidiki
telephone: +30.23740.99 465
website: www.saniresort.gr

Dryades
Agios Lavrentios, Pelion, Magnesia 37300
telephone: +30.24280.96 110/+30.24280.96 224
facsimile: +30.24280.96100
website: pelion-hoteldryades.clickhere.gr/

Erganos Taverna
5 Georgiadi Street, Herakleion
telephone: +30.2810.285 629

Etrusco
Kato Korakiana, Corfu
telephone:+30.26610.93 342

Freudian Oriental
21 Xenokratous Street, Kolonaki, Athens
telephone: +30.210.729 9595

Galaxy Bar
46 Vassilissis Sofias Avenue, Athens 11528
telephone: +30.210.728 1000
facsimile: +30.210.728 1111
email: pr.athens@hilton.com
website: www.hiltonathens.gr

Giorti Baxevannis
End of Iera Odos, Dafni - Xaidari, Athens
telephone: +30.210.532 6163

Hatzis
5 Metropoleos Street, Athens
telephone: +30.210.322 2647
website:www.chatzis.gr

Hilies Kai Dyo Nihtes
10 Karaeskaki Street, Psirri, Athens 10554

I Prasini Akti
Drampatova, Ioannina
telephone: +30. 26510.818 35

Imaret Restaurant
30–32 Theodore Poulidou Street, Kavala 65110
telephone: +30.2510.620 151
facsimile: +30.2510.620 156
email: info@imaret.gr
website: www.imaret.gr

Island Club & Restaurant
7th km of Athens–Sounio Avenue
telephone: +30.210.965 3563/+30.210.965 3564
facsimile: +30.210.892 5053
website: www.islandclubrestaurant.gr

Kafenion
Elounda, Crete 72053
telephone: +30.28410.67 000
facsimile: +30.28410.41 783
email: bay@eloundabay.gr
website: www.eloundabay.gr

Kiriakos
53 Dimokritas Street, Herakleion
telephone: +30.2810.222 464/+30.2810.224 649

Kuzina
9 Adrianou Street, Athens 10555
telephone: +30.210.324 0133
facsimile: +30.210.324 0135
website: www.kuzina.gr

La Bouillabaisse
Agios Nikolaos, Crete 72100
telephone: +30.28410.22 345
facsimile: +30.28410.22 548
email: info-minos@bluegr.com
website: www.bluegr.com

Matsuhisa Athens
40 Apollonos Street, Vouliagmeni, Athens 166 71
telephone: +30.210.896 0510
facsimile: +30.210.896 2520
website: www.astir-palace.com

Matsuhisa Mykonos
School of Fine Arts District, Mykonos 84600
telephone: +30.22890.27 362
facsimile: +30.22890.25 126
email: contact@belvederehotel.com
website: www.belvederehotel.com

Mavri Thalassa
63 An. Thrakis Street, Toumba, Thessaloniki
telephone: +30. 2310.932 542

directory

Meat Me Restaurant
65 Athinas & Lycourgou Street, Athens 10551
telephone: +30.210.325 0900
facsimile: +30.210.325 0920
email: bg@classicalhotels.com
website: www.classicalhotels.com

Milos Restaurant
46 Vassilissis Sofias Avenue, Athens 11528
telephone: +30.210.728 1000
facsimile: +30.210.728 1111
email: pr.athens@hilton.com
website: www.hiltonathens.gr

O Platanos
4 Diogenous Street, Plaka, Athens
telephone: +30.210.322 0666

Ouzaki
58 Psilantou Street, Ladadika, Thessaloniki

Selene Restaurant
Fira, Santorini
telephone: +30.22860.22 249
website: www.selene.gr

Spondi
5 Pyrronos Street, Pagrati Athens 11638
telephone: + 30.210.756 4021
facsimile: +30.210.7 56 7021
email : info@spondi.gr
website: www.spondi.gr

Thalassa
Elounda, Crete 72053
telephone: +30.28410.63 000
facsimile: +30.28410.41 373
email: elohotel@eloundabeach.gr
website: www.eloundabeach.gr

To Kouti
23 Adrianou Street, Monastiraki, Athens
telephone: +30.210.321 3229

Varoulko
80 Piraeus Street, Athens
telephone: +30.210.522 8400
email: info@varoulko.gr
website:www.varoulko.gr

Veghera Club Restaurant
40th Km Athens-Sounion Avenue,
Lagonissi, Athens 19010
telephone: +30.22.9107 6000
facsimile: +30.22.9102 4534
email: reservations@grandresort.gr
website: www.grandresort.gr

Venetian Well
Kremasti Square, Corfu Town 49100
telephone: +30.26610.44 761

Vlassis
8 Paster Street, Mavili Square, Athens
telephone: +30.210.646 3060

Wine Gallery
103 Thisseos Avenue, Ekali, Athens 14578
telephone: +30.210.626 0400
facsimile: +30.210.622 9353
email: info-lifegallery@bluegr.com
website: www.bluegr.com

Zithos
5 Katouni Street, Ladadika, Thessaloniki
telephone : +30.2310.540 284
email : zithos@zithos.gr

Zonar's
Panepistimiou & Voukourestiou streets, Athens
telephone:+30.210.321 1158

GREEK LIBATIONS

A.S. Parparoussis
1, Achilleos Street, Proastio Patron, Patras 26442
telephone:+30.2610.420 334/+30.2610.438 676
facsimile: +30.2610.438 676
email: info@parparoussis.com
website: www.parparoussis.com

Alpha Estate
2nd klm Amyndeon – Agios Panteleimon,
Amyndeon, Athens 53200
telephone: +30.23860.20 111
facsimile: +30.23860.20 132
email: info@alpha-estate.gr
website: www.alpha-estate.gr

Domaine Gerovassiliou
Epanomi, Thessaloniki 57500
telephone: +30.2392.044 567
facsimile: +30.2392.044 560
email: ktima@gerovassiliou.gr
website: www.gerovassiliou.gr

Douloufakis
Dafnes, Heraklion, Crete 70011
telephone: +30.2810.792 017
facsimile: +30.2810.792 260
email: wines@cretanwines.gr
website: www.cretanwines.gr

Estate Hatzimichalis
13th km Athens-Lamia National Road, Nea Kifisia 14564
telephone: +30.210.807 6705
facsimile: +30.210.807 6704
email: info@hatzimichalis.gr
website: www.hatzimichalis.gr

GAIA Estate
22, Themistokleous, Maroussi, Athens 15122
telephone: +30.210.805 5642/+30.210.805 5643
facsimile: +30.210.805 5542
email: gaiawine@otenet.gr
website: www.gaiawines.com

Ktima Biblia Chora
Kokinochori, Kavala 64008
telephone: +30.25920.44 974
facsimile: +30.25920.44 975
email: ktima@bibliachora.gr
website: ktima.bibliachora.gr

Ktima Kir-Yianni
Yianakohori, Naoussa 59200
telephone: +30.23320.51 100
facsimile: +30.23320.51 140
email: info@kiryianni.gr
website: www.kiryianni.gr

Oenoforos
Selinous, Aigio 25100
telephone: +30.26910.29 415
facsimile: +30.26910.60 380
email:info@oenoforos.gr
website:www.oenoforos.gr

GREECE AFTER DARK

Abyssinia Cafe
Plateia Abyssinias, Monastiraki, Athens
telephone: +30.210.321 7047

An Club
13-15 Solomou Street, Exarchia, Athens
telephone: +30.210.330 5056

Aristofanis
Taki Street, Athens

Athens Festival
23 Hadjichristou Street, Athens 11742
telephone: +30.210.928 2900
facsimile: +30.210.928 2941
email: info@greekfestival.gr
website: www.greekfestival.gr

Casino Rodos
4 G Papanikolaou Street, Rhodes Town, Rhodes 85100
telephone: +30.22410.97 500
facsimile: +30.22410.97 504
email: info@casinorodos.gr
website: www.casinorodos.gr

Cubanita Habana Club
28 Karaeskaki Street, Athens
telephone: +30.210.331 4605 - 7
facsimile: +30.210.331 4608
email: mail@cubanita.gr
website: www.cubanita.gr

Distinto Espresso Bar
King George Square, Commercial Centre, Patras
telephone: +30.2610.274 568
website: www.distinto.gr

Frame Lounge Bar
1 Deinokratous Street, Kolonaki, Athens 10675
telephone: +30.210.721 4368
email: info@sglycabettus.gr
website: www.sgl-frame.gr

Harama
Mezonos & Kapodistriou streets, Patras

Hotel Belvedere, Mykonos
School of Fine Arts District, Mykonos 84600
telephone: +30.22890.25 122
facsimile: +30.22890.25 126
email: contact@belvederehotel.com
website: www.belvederehotel.com

House of Art
4 Saktouri Street, Athens

Hytra
7 Navarxou Apostoli Street, Psirri, Athens
telephone: +30.210.331 6767

Koo Club
Fira, Santorini
telephone: +30.22860.22 025
email: koo@kooclub.gr
website: www.kooclub.gr/

Mamacas
41 Persephone Street, Athens 11854
telephone: +30.210.346 4984
email: mamakas@otenet.gr
website: www.mamacas.gr

Megaron Mousikis concert hall
Vassilissis Sofias Avenue and Kokkali Street,
Athens 11521
telephone: +30.210.728 2333
website: www.megaron.gr

National Theatre of Greece
22 Aghiou Konstantinou Street, Athens 10473
website: www.n-t.gr

Nipiagogeio
8, Elasidon & Kleanthous streets, Athens 11854
telephone: +30.210.345 8534

Notos
80 Patreos Street, Patras
telephone: +30.2610.621 181

Rempétiki Istoria
181 Ippokratous Street, Neapolis, Athens 11472
telephone: +30.210.642 4937
website: rempetiki-istoria.com/English

The Greek National Opera
59-61 Academias Street, Athens
telephone: +30.210.361 2461/+30.210.364 3725
facsimile: +30.36.43 577
email: pr@nationalopera.gr
website: www.nationalopera.gr

A YACHTING ODYSSEY

eYachtCharter.com
website: www.eyachtcharter.com

Hellenic Charters
Aristofanous Street, Glyfada 16674
telephone: +30.210.963 6602
email: charters@hellenic-charters.com
website: www.hellenic-charters.gr

Hellenic Offshore Racing Club
3 Akti Athinas Dilaveri, Mikrolimano, Pireaus 18533
email: info@horc.gr
website: www.horc.gr/en

National Geographic Expeditions
website: www.nationalgeographicalexpeditions.com

Smithsonian Journeys
website: www.smithsonianjourneys.com

The Moorings
website: www.moorings.com

Yacht Club of Greece
18 Karageorgi Servias Street, Pireaus 18533
telephone: +30.210.417 9730
facsimile: +30.210.412 4177
website: www.ycg.gr